100
WOMEN
WHO SHAPED WORLD HISTORY

Gail Meyer Rolka

A Bluewood Book

This edition was produced and published in 1994 by Bluewood Books
A division of The Siyeh Group, Inc.,
38 South B Street, Suite 202
San Mateo, CA 94401

ISBN 0-912517-06-9

Printed in USA

Designed and
captioned by Tom Debolski

Cover illustration by
Vadim Vahrameev

Key to front cover illustration:
1. Cleopatra VII
2. Susan Brownell Anthony
3. Eleanor Roosevelt
4. Indira Gandhi
5. Queen Victoria
6. Amelia Earhart
7. Florence Nightingale
8. Marian Anderson

About the Author:
Gail Meyer Rolka has a masters degree in Social Work and worked for 15 years in the field of Child Welfare. For the past eight years, she has been involved in the publishing industry. She lives in Novato, California, with her husband, two children and two cats. This is her first book.

Acknowledgments:
The author wishes to thank her daughter Adrienne for her help as a research assistant and her husband Jim for his support throughout this project; and Garlyn Peterson, Paul Focht, Lynne Piade and Rich Michaels for their help in securing research materials.

TABLE OF CONTENTS

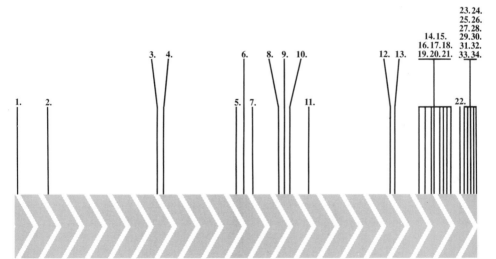

1500 BC   1AD   1800AD

35. CATHERINE BEECHER *42* 1800-1878	52. MARY HARRIS JONES (MOTHER JONES) *59* 1830-1930
36. DOROTHEA DIX *43* 1802-1887	53. LOUISA MAY ALCOTT *60* 1832-1888
37. HARRIET BEECHER STOWE *44* 1811-1896	54. SOPHIA JEX-BLAKE *61* 1840-1912
38. ADA LOVELACE *45* 1815-1852	55. ANNIE BESANT *62* 1847-1933
39. CHARLOTTE BRONTË 1816-1855	56. EMMA LAZARUS *63* 1849-1887
40. and EMILY BRONTË 1818-1848 *46*	
41. ELIZABETH CADY STANTON *48* 1815-1902	57. EMMELINE PANKHURST 1858-1928
42. LUCY STONE *49* 1818-1893	58. and CHRISTABEL PANKHURST 1880-1958 *64*
43. MARY ANN EVANS (GEORGE ELIOT) *50* 1819-1880	59. CARRIE CHAPMAN CATT *66* 1859-1947
44. QUEEN VICTORIA *51* 1819-1901	60. JANE ADDAMS *67* 1860-1935
45. SUSAN BROWNELL ANTHONY *52* 1820-1906	61. MARY KINGSLEY *68* 1862-1900
46. FLORENCE NIGHTINGALE 53 1820-1910	62. MARIE CURIE *69* 1867-1934
47. HARRIET TUBMAN *54* c. 1820-1913	63. SARAH BREEDLOVE WALKER *70* 1867-1919
48. CLARA BARTON *55* 1821-1912	64. GERTRUDE BELL *71* 1868-1926
49. ELIZABETH BLACKWELL *56* 1821-1910	65. ALICE HAMILTON *72* 1869-1970
50. MARY BAKER EDDY *57* 1821-1910	66. ROSA LUXEMBURG *73* 1870-1919
51. LAKSHMI BAI, RANI OF JHANSI *58* c. 1830-1858	67. MARIA MONTESSORI *74* 1870-1952
	68. JULIA MORGAN *75* 1872-1957

1800 AD   1850   1900

84. 85.   89. 90.   93. 94. 96.

86. 87. 88.   91. 92.   95. 97. 98. 99.   100.

1900   1950   2000

INTRODUCTION

When anthropologists discuss prehistoric humankind, they usually focus their attention on the role played by "man the hunter," ignoring, or de-emphasizing, the more pivotal role of "woman the food gatherer." Gathering—not hunting—was the primary survival activity of our ancestors, and this role was almost exclusively performed by women who developed the tools and technology needed to acquire, prepare and preserve foods. At first using simple implements such as sticks and flints for digging roots, women later invented the mortar and pestle and a rudimentary mill for grinding grains and seeds.

Around 12,000 BC, an agricultural revolution took place when humans progressed from being gatherers and hunters to farmers. This transition was facilitated by women gatherers who over time cultivated wild plants and developed new edible foods. In the Tigris and Euphrates valleys of Mesopotamia, women domesticated barley, flax, and wheat from wild grasses, in China they raised rice and in North America potatoes and maize (corn). The heritage of these early women was kept alive by oral history.

After the invention of the wheel (c. 3500 BC), technology advanced dramatically. By 1100 BC, the invention of devices such as the potter's wheel and metal tools transformed the manufacture of household goods and created a new class of specialized craftspeople and merchants. With planned agriculture, industry and trade flourished, and eventually societies developed written languages. However, once agriculture was undertaken on a large scale, women's role in food production was taken over by men. As humankind entered the era of written history, the accomplishments of men—not those of women—were noted for posterity.

Women as the preparers of food.

Until the late twentieth century, the recorded history of Western societies was overwhelmingly dominated by the exploits of men. With rare exceptions, information contained in traditional reference works, such as encyclopedias and history books, showed a definite bias toward the contributions of men while overlooking or downplaying those of women. For instance, though many women scientists were recognized and respected in their day, later historians tended to discredit their contributions, or, because women often did not publish under their own names, failed to recognize their efforts. Such was the case with **Marie Lavoisier**, whose 25 years of collaboration with her husband laid the groundwork for modern chemistry, and **Emilie du Chatelet**, a Newtonian scientist who greatly influenced the work of her companion, **Voltaire**. And what history text has given **Catherine Greene** credit for co-inventing the cotton gin with **Eli Whitney**?

Women, in fact, have not just kept the home fires burning and raised children for the past 5000 years. They have also advanced technology, discovered new lands, created innovative art, music and dance, led armies, added to the body of important world literature, become influential national leaders, and questioned and changed existing social beliefs and structures to improve the quality of life for all people. To do so, many had to overcome formidable obstacles. Barred from entering a university, mathematician **Sophie Germain** borrowed lecture notes, taught herself and formulated a prize-winning theory. Without any formal education at all, **Madame C.J. Walker** started her own company and became the first self-made woman millionaire in America.

Many women made their mark in history by challenging society to provide equal rights for all citizens, often sacrificing their personal lives to reach this goal. **Dorothea Dix** and **Elizabeth Fry** crusaded for prison reform. **Emmeline Pankhurst** and her daughters spearheaded the drive for women's suffrage in England. In America, **Susan B. Anthony** and **Carrie Chapman Catt**, among others, devoted their lives to securing voting rights for women. As Catt calculated it, it took activists 51 years of continual effort—including 56 referenda to male voters, 480 submissions to state legislatures, 277 campaigns to obtain backing from state party conventions, 47 efforts to persuade state constitutional conventions, 30 campaigns to influence presidential parties, and 19 successive campaigns with 19 consecutive Congresses—to gain the vote.

This book contains biographical sketches that celebrate the lives and achievements of 100 unique, talented women who lived in many parts of the globe during various eras of history from 1500 BC to the present. Some—such as **Eleanor Roosevelt** and **Queen Victoria**—are household names. Others—such as **Zenobia** and **Sophia Jex-Blake**—will not be as familiar. But all the women in this book have one thing in common: they helped shape the history of the world around them. Though the influence of some was primarily confined to their own lifetimes, the legacy of others, like that of **Queen Jinga** of Angola, survives today as an inspiration to a whole new generation.

Women have done much more than keep the home fires burning and raise children for the past 5000 years.

1. QUEEN MAKARE HATSHEPSUT
d. 1483 BC

Queen Makare Hatshepsut (mä-kă′rə hät′shĕp′ sōot) of the eighteenth dynasty is not only remembered for her reign of peace and prosperity during which trade flourished, but for her glorious mortuary temple—called the **Sublime of the Sublimes**—that was built into the cliffs at Der el-Bahri opposite the temple of Karnak at Thebes. Its walls, inscribed with a pictorial account of the events of her life and their divine origin, are the source of most present-day knowledge about her.

Hatshepsut was the daughter of **Thutmose I** (thōot-mō′sə) by his sister and major queen **Ahmose** (ä-mo′sə). His successor, **Thutmose II**, his son by a lesser queen, followed Egyptian tradition and married his half-sister Hatshepsut, who had only daughters. His heir, **Thutmose III** was born of the union with his lesser wife **Isis**. When Hatshepsut's husband died, she

Queen Hatshepsut with her attendants.

became the ruler for six-year-old Thutmose III, and in 1503 BC she assumed the double crown, taking the title of pharaoh herself. Once on the throne, she announced that **Amon-Ra** (ä-mŭn Ră) the king of the gods, had chosen her to rule. To further strengthen her position, she appointed as advisors the most eminent and talented men of her kingdom. One such man was **Senenmut** (sĕ-nĕn′mŭt), her chief of works and a close confidante who became a "foster father" and tutor to her daughters. At her direction, he restored the temple of the goddess Hathor at Cusae that had fallen into ruin. He also designed and built her magnificent mortuary temple at Der el-Bahri, which he placed on top of a series of three terraces each flanked by porticoes that were supported by fluted columns. A double column of sphinxes led up to the lower terrace, where two four-sided stone pillars with pyramid-shaped tops were placed.

Under Hatshepsut, trade was resumed with neighboring Negau, from which she obtained timber, and the turquoise mines of the Sinai were reopened. She also sent envoys south to negotiate trade agreements for metals and other commodities, such as panther skins and elephant tusks from coastal Libya. One of the most remarkable events in her reign was the expedition to Punt that established a route down the Nile and overland to the Red Sea to obtain incense trees, whose grains were burned before statues of the pharaohs. Thirty-one trees were planted in front of the terraces at Der el-Bahri.

When Thutmose III ascended the throne, he smashed the statues at Hatshepsut's beautiful temple and buried the pieces. Over 3400 years later, archaeologists from the New York Museum of Science retrieved many of the fragments and painstakingly restored them.

2. DEBORAH
c. 1150 BC

Known as the **Mother of Israel**, prophetess and judge **Deborah** (dĕb'ər-ə) rallied the tribes of Israel to defeat the Canaanite king **Jabin** and his military commander **Sisera** on the great plain of Jezreel by the Kishon River near Megiddo circa 1150 BC. This victory welded together Israel's autonomous and scattered tribes—**Issachar, Zebulon** and **Naphtali** from the north and Ephraim, Benjamin and Machir-Mannasseh from the south—with the unifying element of religion, and led to 40 years of peace.

This story is vividly dramatized in the magnificent triumphal ode *The Song of Deborah* in chapter five of the **Book of Judges** in the Old Testament of the Bible.

Biblical "judges" were the freedom fighters of their era, renowned not only for their wise legal and religious judgments but for their military leadership. When the people of Israel fell away from Yahweh and were delivered into bondage or hardship, He would send a judge to lead them to victory and back to the practice of their religion.

Deborah, the only woman judge among many men, was the wife of **Lapidoth** and came from the tribe of Issachar, which dwelled between Bethel and Ramah in the hill country of Ephraim. The Israelite tribes generally inhabited the mountainous highlands while the Canaanites, with their chariots, calvary and strategic fortifications at Tannach, Megiddo and Bethsehan, controlled the plains and mountain passes through which caravan routes ran.

Deborah summoned **Barak** and instructed him to raise an army of 10,000 to meet Sisera in battle. Barak was unwilling to go unless she accompanied him, which she did, predicting that "the Lord will hand Sisera over to a woman." (Judges 4:9). The Israelites successfully routed their enemy and Sisera fled on foot to the neighboring

Deborah.

settlement of **Heber the Kenite**, which was friendly to King Jabin. Seeking refuge in Heber's tent, he was killed with a tent peg by Heber's wife **Jael** (yä-ĕl) while he slept, thus fulfilling Deborah's prophecy. (Judges 4:21).

To commemorate this event, Deborah (or possibly a contemporary) composed *The Song of Deborah*. The oldest surviving piece of Biblical writing and the most elaborate of all early war songs, it is viewed by scholars as a masterpiece of Jewish poetry and is considered one of the finest odes in the literature of the world. The ode, sung by Deborah at the annual festival following the victory when people offered gifts of thanksgiving to Yahweh, is also a document of great historical importance for our knowledge of the history of Israel. It is also unique for the fact that two women—Deborah and Jael—appear as its heroines.

3. SAPPHO (PSAPPHO)
c. 625-570 BC

Born in Mytilene on the Greek island of Lesbos, **Sappho** (or **Psappho**, as she called herself), was so renowned as a poet that two centuries after her death **Plato (427-347 BC)** referred to her as "the tenth muse." Although what is known about her life and work comes from fragments recorded by others, it appears that Sappho was one of four children born to a wealthy family, was married at an early age to Cercylas and had a daughter whom she named Cleis after her own mother. She was a contemporary of **Aesop** (ē′səp), King **Croesus** (krē′səs) and lyric poets **Stesichorus** (stə-sī′kôr-əs)and **Alcaeus** (ăl-sē-əs). She and Alcaeus were the first to write personal, subjective prose, a form that is still popular today.

According to **Tullius Laurea**, Sappho wrote nine books of odes, epithalamia (wedding songs), elegies and hymns, but surviving fragments are few. The nine books appear to be arranged according to the meter of their poetry. Book one, for instance, contains pieces written only in **Sapphics**, a form of verse she invented. These verses consist of a four-line stanza in which the first three lines are each 11 syllables long and the fourth stanza is five syllables long.

Sappho.

While other poets glorified gods and heroes, Sappho's poems most commonly were about love, death and passion and were filled with idyllic scenes from Greek life and the lives of women. Surviving fragments of her poetry include *The Ode of Aphrodite*, which was quoted by scholar **Dionysius of Halicarnassus** (dī′ə-nĭsh′ē-əs hăl′ĭ-kär-näs′əs) in the first century BC. The work of many later Greek poets, including **Theocritus** (thē-ŏk′rĕ-təs) **(c. 310-250 BC)**, bear the mark of her influence.

Sappho taught music and poetry to a group of aristocratic young women, and when they would marry, she composed a special ode for the occasion. She also invented a 21-string lyre that she used to accompany herself when she sang her poems.

Sappho's writings were acclaimed for their beautiful diction, extreme simplicity of form and great depth and intensity of emotion, which made her poems unique. In contrast to other poets of her time, the language she used was not an artificially-created literary dialect but rather ordinary speech, as shown in this poem about death: "We know this much/Death is an evil/We have the gods'/Word for it; they too/Would die if death/Were a good thing."

Writing about **Aspasia** (ăs-pā′zhə) over 2000 years after her death, American president **John Adams (1735-1826)** said, "I wish some of our great men had such wives." Aspasia lived during one of the greatest ages in the history of the world when classical civilizations flourished in ancient Greece and Rome. From this era we can recall many famous men such as philosophers **Socrates** (sŏk′ə-tēz′) **(c. 470-399 BC)** and **Plato (c. 427-347 BC)** and playwright **Euripedes** (yŏŏ-rĭp′ĭ-dēz′) **(484-406 BC)**. However, much less has been recorded about their female contemporaries because women were usually relegated to the roles of slaves, courtesans or wives, who were confined to home and excluded from participation in public life.

Aspasia, who was born in Miletus in eastern Greece, arrived in Athens around 450 BC. Being a foreigner, by law she was not allowed to marry, so she became one of a group of women known as *hetaerae*—female companions who were highly educated and, because they were single, were free to study, attend lectures and even engage in debates with men.

Known for her genius and great beauty, Aspasia opened a school of philosophy and rhetoric. Soon her home became the most popular salon in Athens, frequented by leading scholars, politicians and artists, including Plato, who said she taught him his theory of love, and Socrates, who credited her with teaching him the art of eloquence. Also in attendance was **Pericles** (pĕr-ĕ-klēz) **(495-429 BC)**, Athens' chief magistrate. His 30-year administration, later known as the **Age of Pericles**, was a time when Athens became a democratic state and reigned as the intellectual and artistic center of the country.

Pericles fell in love with Aspasia, but since she was not of Athenian birth and therefore could not legally become his wife, he divorced his wife and made her his consort. From then on, Aspasia acted as his political advisor and confidante, supporting him in his struggle against the aristocracy to establish a democracy. Some historians hold her responsible for the disastrous **Peloponnesian War** (pĕl′ə-pə-nē′zhən) **(431 BC)**, which they believe Pericles waged at her urging. Others give her credit for writing the eloquent speech he delivered to his troops at the conclusion of this war. Aspasia also lobbied Pericles to change laws that restricted women's roles in Greek society.

After the death of his two sons by his wife, Pericles enacted a law making Pericles, his son by Aspasia, an Athenian citizen. Young Pericles later became an army general. Unable to criticize Pericles directly, Athenians angry over his relationship with Aspasia charged her with acting disrespectful toward the gods. After an impassioned, tearful defense by Pericles, she was found innocent.

Aspasia.

A beautiful and politically ambitious woman, **Cleopatra VII** was the daughter of **Ptolemy XI Auletes** (tŏl′ə-me ô-lē′təs) **(112-51 BC)**, king of Egypt. Her father died when she was 17, and by custom she was wed to her 12-year-old brother, **Ptolemy XII (63-47 BC)**. They began a joint rule in 51 BC but Ptolemy, prompted by advisors, seized total control and drove his sister into exile. She met the Roman General **Gaius Julius Caesar** (gī′əs jōōl′yəs sē′zər) **(100-44 BC)** in Alexandria, who became enamored of her. He undertook a war on her behalf against her brother, in which Ptolemy was killed, and he then declared Cleopatra to be queen of Egypt.

Following her required marriage to her 11-year-old brother **Ptolemy XIII (59-44 BC)**, Cleopatra accompanied Caesar to Rome. He had a gold statue built in her honor and provided her with a luxurious

Cleopatra VII.

villa near the Tiber River, where she gave birth to their son **Caesarion (47-30 BC)**. When Caesar was assassinated in 44 BC, she returned to Egypt, poisoned her brother and ascended the throne, installing her young son as her co-ruler.

Shortly after this, **Marcus Antonius (Mark Antony, 82-30 BC)**, the commander of the Eastern Roman Empire, summoned Cleopatra to Rome for a meeting. He fell in love with her and followed her back to Egypt where they lived together for several years and had two daughters. Antony was recalled to Rome to marry Octavia, a sister of Caesar's great-nephew and heir **Augustus (Gaius Octavian, 63 BC-14 AD)**, but in 36 BC he returned to the east as the commander of an expedition against the Parthians, at which time he sent for Cleopatra and they were reunited at Antioch. Beyond their legendary love affair, the union of Antony and Cleopatra was a political act that united all of Rome against Antony. Angry at Antony's affair and fearful that he and Cleopatra planned to take control of the eastern half of the Roman Empire, Octavian declared war against them in 32 BC.

At the naval battle at **Actium** in 31 BC, believing defeat was inevitable, Cleopatra withdrew her fleet, and she and Antony fled to Alexandria. Receiving a false report that Cleopatra had already committed suicide, Antony killed himself. When Cleopatra learned Octavian planned to exhibit her in Rome as proof of his triumph, she committed suicide by taking poison, although another traditional story says she died from the bite of an asp.

As a result, Octavian killed Antony and Cleopatra's son, Caesarion, who was the last of the Ptolemy dynasty, and he turned Egypt into a Roman province. Octavian then became the first sole ruler of the Roman Empire and reigned until his death in 14 AD.

6. MARY, THE MOTHER OF JESUS CHRIST c. 22-20 BC

All historical knowledge about the life of **Mary** is contained in the **Gospels** written by the apostles **Matthew, Luke** and **John**, which are part of the New Testament of the Bible. According to Christian belief, **Jesus Christ**—the son of God born on earth in human form—was the Messiah who had come to free the people of Israel from the bonds of Roman rule and lead them to a new kingdom. As Jesus' mother, Mary occupies an important role in the theology and worship of many of the world's 1.6 billion Christians, particularly those in the Catholic Church.

Historians estimate that Mary was between 16 and 18 years old at the time of her son's birth in 4 BC. However, the precise circumstances of her death are unknown and the Gospels provide only brief glimpses of her life. She belonged to the house of David (Luke 1:26), lived in lower Galilee (Luke 1:26) and became engaged to a carpenter named Joseph (Matthew 1:18).

The angel Gabriel told her that though a virgin, she would conceive the son of God (Luke 1:26). In Luke 1:39, Mary visited her cousin Elizabeth and recited the Magnificat ("My soul doth magnify the Lord...") She was a silent presence at her son's birth and the visits of the shepherds and Magi (Matthew 1:12; Luke 2:1) and when Jesus was presented at the temple (Luke 2:21). Later, when she finds him teaching at the temple, she utters the second of three recorded statements: "My son, why have you acted so with us? Your father and I have looked for you in sorrow" (Luke 2:41). Her last recorded statement was at the marriage feast at Cana when she told Jesus "They have no wine," prompting him to perform his first miracle of changing water into wine (John 2:1). She is last seen at the foot of the cross weeping when Jesus dies (John 19:25).

Mary with the baby Jesus.

Known from scriptures as the **Virgin Mary**, Christians soon began to honor Mary as the **Mother of God—Theotokos** (thē-ŏt′əkəs). By the seventh century, they came to believe she had remained a virgin all her life (**Ever Virgin**). In the Middle Ages, Mary's perpetual purity came to imply she was free from all sin, including original sin, later defined in Roman Catholic dogma as the **Immaculate Conception** (1854). In 1950, Pope Pius XII decreed that Mary, at the end of her earthly life, had been assumed into heaven, body and soul.

Mary's reported appearances in succeeding years to fervent believers on earth has led to the building of shrines in her honor around the world, the most famous of which are the **Black Madonna of Czestochowa** (chĕn′stə-kō′və) (Poland), revered since the fourteenth century; the picture of **Our Lady of Guadalupe** (gwäd′lōōpē) commemorating an appearance in Mexico in 1531; **Our Lady of Lourdes** (lŏŏrds) (France, 1858); and **Our Lady of Fatima** (Portugal, 1917).

Boadicea (bō'ăd-ĭsē'ə) became queen of the **Iceni** tribe in 60 AD upon the death of her husband King **Prasutagus**, who had ruled what is now Norfolk and Sussex counties in England as a client king under the jurisdiction of the Roman Emperor **Nero (37-68 AD)**. Prasutagus tried to insure imperial protection for his family by leaving a will that divided his lands equally between his two daughters and Nero. However, after his death, Nero immediately annexed all of his lands. His soldiers tortured Boadicea and assaulted her daughters, and enslaved the Iceni tribesmen.

Enraged, the proud queen called her countrymen together to expel the Roman invaders, amassing a native force of over 100,000, including women and children. For many years, Roman taxation in East Anglia had been extremely burdensome, and the cruel suppression of the Iceni was the catalyst for action. With the Roman Governor General **Suetonius Paulinus** and his troops away fighting Druids in north Wales, a favorable situation existed for a full-scale revolt.

The Britons destroyed the Roman colony at Camulodunum (now Colchester), sacked Londinium (London), burned the tribal capital of Veralamium (St. Albans) and leveled several military outposts. According to historian **Cornelius Tacitus (c. 55-120 AD)**, Boadicea's forces killed some 70,000 Roman soldiers and British sympathizers and nearly annihilated the Ninth Roman Legion that was marching from Lincoln to provide reinforcements.

Returning with 10,000 soldiers, Suetonius met the Britons in the field near Fenny in Stratford. Boadicea herself rode into battle on a chariot accompanied by her two daughters. Several days of fierce combat turned into one of the worst slaughters in British history, with the Romans killing 80,000 Britons—nearly one-tenth of all Celts in England. To prevent being captured, Boadicea took poison.

As a result of Boadicea's revolt, the Roman government adopted a fairer policy of governing Britain and Suetonius was replaced by a more reasonable governor. Nero, who had levied huge taxes to rebuild Rome and indulged in murderous excesses toward suspected enemies, was condemned to die by the Roman Senate. Prior to being executed, he committed suicide.

In 1902, a memorial statue of Boadicea, clutching a spear as she commands a chariot pulled by two rearing horses, was erected near the Westminster Bridge over the Thames River, facing the Houses of Parliament in London. Inscribed on its base are the words: "Regions Caesar never knew/ Thy Posterity shall sway."

Boadicea.

Although it is **Constantine the Great (c. 274-337 AD)** who is given credit for establishing **Christianity** as the dominant religion of the Western world, it was the influence and good works of his mother, **Helena**, which served to greatly expedite the spread of the faith. Some historians even contend that Helena became a Christian before her son and was responsible for his conversion. Others, citing the number of churches she founded, consider her to be the **Mother of Christianity**.

Helena was born in Drepanum in the ancient Roman province of Bithynia on the Nicomedian Gulf. The daughter of an innkeeper, she met **Constantius (d. 306 AD)** when he passed through her district while engaged in a military conquest. After 19 years together, during which time she gave birth to her only son, Constantine, Constantius abandoned her when he became ruler of the **Roman Empire** so he could marry the stepdaughter of his patron, Emperor **Maximanius Herculius**.

After his father died in 306 AD and Constantine succeeded him as emperor, he summoned Helena to his court in Rome and conferred on her the title of Augusta, dowager empress. To further honor his mother, he renamed her birthplace **Helenopolis** and had her likeness imprinted on coins.

Helena, who was very religiously devout, made a pilgrimage to the Holy Land and visited Jerusalem in 324 AD. Excavating beneath the rubble of a pagan temple, she found pieces of wood that she claimed were remnants of the true cross on which Jesus Christ had been crucified three centuries before. On this site, she founded the **Church of the Holy Sepulchre**. She then traveled to Bethlehem to locate Jesus' birthplace and built the **Church of the Nativity** on what she believed to be the site. Although these sites have never been historically authenticated and are at best educated guesses on Helena's part, the churches still draw thousands of pilgrims annually.

After founding many more churches, Helena rejoined her son, who had moved his capital from Rome to Constantinople, and she died there at the age of 80. Immediately upon her death, she was revered as a saint. Constantine had her buried in the imperial vault of the Church of the Apostles, but around 849 AD, her body was transferred to the **Abbey of Hautvillers**, near Rheims, France, where her resting place continues to be a place of pilgrimage. In the Roman Catholic church her feast day is celebrated as August 18. In the Eastern Orthodox church her feast day is celebrated jointly with that of her son on May 21.

The Church of the Holy Sepulchre.

9. ZENOBIA (SEPTIMIA BAT ZABBAI)
c. 3rd century AD

A brilliant and ambitious woman, **Zenobia** (zĕ'nō-bē'ə) (native name: **Septimia Bat Zabbai**) was born in the desert city of Palmyra in present-day Syria, the daughter of a wealthy Arab merchant. Her military quest to make Palmyra supreme in the eastern region of the Roman Empire made her a heroine of her time.

The opulent city of Palmyra lay at the crossroads of vital caravan routes between Rome and Persia. Zenobia's husband, **Odainat (d. 266 AD)**, ruled it as a client king of Rome. After Roman Emperor **Valerian** was murdered by King **Sopor I** of Persia in 260 AD, Odainat, hoping to increase his stature with Rome, crushed Persia. Zenobia, who often hunted panther and other game with her husband and disdained a chariot in favor of a horse, accompanied him. After his death in 266, she decided to extend his conquests to make Palmyra the undisputed power in the region.

Rather than ruling on behalf of her son **Vaballathus Athenodorus**, Zenobia ascended the throne and declared herself Queen of the East. She immediately attacked Egypt while the armies of Rome were fighting a barbarian invasion of Italy, and by 269 AD, most of Egypt fell to her general **Zabadas**. She then annexed a majority of Syria, and by 270 she had extended her domain into Asia Minor as far as Bithynia on the Bosphorus Strait. She now not only controlled commerce vital to Rome, but also the trade routes with Abyssinia, Arabia and India.

Declaring herself independent of Rome, Zenobia ruled an empire that was founded on tolerance rather than persecution. She established cordial relations with Jews at Alexandria as well as with **Paul**, the Christian Bishop of Antioch. For the brief while her court flourished, it became known for its intellectual distinction as well as its extravagant show of wealth.

Zenobia.

When Emperor **Lucius Domitius Aurelian (c. 212-275 AD)** came to power in 270 AD, he recognized the threat that Zenobia posed to the unity of the Roman Empire. Within a year, he had retaken Egypt and Asia Minor and lay siege to Palmyra itself. Zenobia and her son escaped the city only to be captured boarding a boat at Euphrates on their way to seek support from Persia. After parading her through the streets of Rome bedecked in jewels as a symbol of his conquest, Aurelian set her free. She later married a Roman senator and retired in affluent luxury to a villa at Tibur (now Tivoli), where she opened a fashionable salon.

Shortly before his death in 275 AD, Aurelian was compelled to return to Palmyra to quell another insurrection. This time the city was plundered, and its civilization disappeared in the desert sands.

10. HYPATIA
370-415 AD

Known as the first woman mathematician, **Hypatia** (hī-pā′shə) was also a philosopher, scientist and scholar. Born in Alexandria, she was raised by her father **Theon** after her mother died when she was a baby. A university mathematics professor and noted astronomer, he supervised every aspect of Hypatia's education. Under his tutelage, she studied mathematics, science, literature, philosophy and the arts, while also engaging in a vigorous daily routine of exercise with him.

After attending a school in Athens taught by **Plutarch (46-120 AD)**, Hypatia returned to Alexandria and became a professor at the university, where she is said to have occupied the chair of Platonic philosophy. Hypatia was considered something of an oracle, and students from many areas of the country were drawn to Alexandria to hear her inspired lectures on mathematics and to study with her.

Most of what we know about Hypatia today comes from letters she wrote to one

Hypatia.

A sixteenth-century astrolabe

of her pupils, **Synesius of Cyrene** in Greece, who later became bishop of Ptolemais in 411. Hypatia suggested that Synesius measure the positions of stars and planets with an **astrolabe** and a **planisphere**, astronomical instruments that she had designed.

Hypatia, who retained her Greek religious traditions though Christianity was becoming dominant in Alexandria, is believed to have become a victim of a power struggle between her friend **Orestes**, the Roman prefect of Egypt, and **Cyril**, the Christian patriarch of Alexandria who was committed to eliminating what he viewed as heretical religious beliefs. Inflamed by Cyril, a mob kidnapped and murdered her in 415 AD.

Some historians view Hypatia's death as marking the end of the golden age of Greek mathematics. Two hundred years later, Alexandria was destroyed by the Arabs, ending a thousand-year tradition of state-of-the-art academics at the University at Alexandria.

11. THEODORA
497-548 AD

As described by Byzantine historian **Procopius** (prə-kō′pə-əs) **(c. 500-565 AD)** in his book *Secret History (Anecdota)*, **Theodora** was the daughter of **Acadious**, the bear-keeper at the Hippodrome in Constantinople. Orphaned at age four, she joined her sister in the theater. By age 15, she was a well-known dancer and mime who was renowned for her beauty and comedic talents. On her travels through Egypt, she encountered **Timothy**, a **Monophysite** (mə-nŏf′ə-sīt′) (one who believed that Jesus Christ had a composite nature that was both human and divine) who greatly influenced her religious education.

While working as a wool spinner in Constantinople, Theodora met **Justinian I (483-565 AD)**, heir to the Byzantine throne, who was 20 years her senior, and he fell in love with her. In 523, his uncle, **Justin I (452-527 AD)**, repealed the law which forbade the marriage of senators and women of the stage, and they were wed.

Upon his uncle's death, Justinian ascended the throne and made Theodora his co-ruler. Her skill and authority immediately became evident in all facets of administrative, religious and political affairs. Early on in their joint reign, as a result of high taxes and other political conflicts, an insurrection known as the **Nika Revolt** (532 AD) broke out in Constantinople. Theodora convinced her husband not to flee the city when the rebels were attacking the palace, which allowed his troops, commanded by his general **Belisarius**, to disperse the rioters.

Although totally committed to her husband's vision of rebuilding the Roman Empire, Theodora remained opposed to expanding their holdings by continual warfare. History has shown her view to be the wiser choice. Justinian is most well known for his codification of Roman law, a process which took 10 years, and Theodora

Justinian and Theodora.

exerted a great deal of influence on his thinking. The result of his work, the *Codex* and other volumes, still form the basis of the legal systems in many European countries.

Theodora's devotion to social justice for women was unique for her time. During her reign, divorce laws were modified, daughters were allowed to inherit, wives allowed to retain their dowries as their own property, and children could not be sold as slaves to pay off their parents' debts. An edict in 535 outlawed brothels in the major cities and Theodora, at her own expense, purchased the freedom of 500 girls who had been sold into prostitution and provided a house for them near the Black Sea.

After she died of cancer at the age of 51, Justinian was so distraught that little effective legislation was passed during the remaining 17 years of his life.

12. ELEANOR OF AQUITAINE
1122-1204

As queen of France (1137-1152), queen of England (1154-1204) and the mother of two English kings, **Richard I (1157-1199, called Richard the Lion-Hearted)** and **John I (1167-1216), Eleanor of Aquitaine** (ăk′wĭ-tān′) was one of the most politically influential women of her time. Born in France, the daughter of **William X** of Aquitaine, she was wed to King **Louis VII** of France in 1137. During 15 years of marriage, she bore two daughters and accompanied her husband on the **Second Crusade** to the Holy Land between 1147 and 1149, taking with her 300 women both to fight and to nurse the wounded. By mutual consent, their marriage was annulled in 1152.

Besieged by suitors, Eleanor married Henry Plantagenet, count of Anjou, who in 1154 became King **Henry II (1133-1189)**, the first Plantagenet king of England, and she subsequently bore him five sons and three daughters. She brought to the marriage the extensive Duchy of Aquitaine, Gascony and Poitiers—which she had inherited from her father at age 15—an event that marks the beginning of the conflict between France and England which continued throughout the **Middle Ages**. In 1170, she convinced Henry to invest their son Richard with these lands.

Henry's continued unfaithfulness alienated Eleanor, so when her sons Richard and John rebelled against their father in 1173, she sided with them. After they were unsuccessful in their attempt to overthrow their father, she was captured while attempting to flee and imprisoned until her husband's death in 1189. Once released, she became a powerful presence at court, granting amnesty to prisoners and securing the succession of her son Richard to the throne. She ruled on his behalf during his absence on the **Third Crusade**, thwarting an attempt by John to conspire with France against England. Upon Richard's return in 1194, she negotiated a reconciliation between the two brothers, which served to maintain peace in England and insure John's succession to the throne.

Eleanor's influence also extended to culture and education. In both England and France, where she reigned as queen for a total of 65 years, she gathered leading poets, scholars and musicians at her courts and founded educational institutions. In her eighties, she arranged the marriage of her grand-daughter **Blanche of Castile** to King **Louis VIII** of France and successfully defended her French territories against assaults. Through the marriages of her five daughters, she created alliances with several ruling houses in Europe. She retired to the Abbey of Fontrevault, France in 1201, where she died at the age of 82.

Eleanor of Aquitaine.

Beloved by the people of her country, **Tamara (Thamar)**, the great medieval queen of Georgia, brought her kingdom to the peak of its glory before the Mongol hoards of **Genghis Khan** (gĕng′gĕs kän) **(c. 1167- 1227)** destroyed its capital of Tiflis (now Tbilisi) in 1236. The memory of the golden age she helped create still lives on today in Georgian myths and history.

The feudal kingdom of Georgia was located in a pivotal position on the crossroads between Europe, China and the Middle East. It was bounded on the west by the Black Sea; on the east by the Caspian Sea, across which lay Persia, India and Central Asia; on the north by the Caucasus Mountains, a barricade against Russia; and on the south by Armenia's mountainous plateau, a buffer against the Turkish Empire. Georgia was converted to Christianity in the fourth century, and in the eighth century the house of Bagrationi first gained the throne, later reaching its height under Tamara's great-grandfather, King **David II** (known as the **Restorer, 1089-1125**). However, his heirs lost much territory to invading Muslims.

Six years before his death, Tamara's father, King **Giorgi III (d. 1184)** crowned her as his co-ruler in 1178, giving her the title of "Mountain of God." To fulfill her duty of producing an heir, in 1187 she married **Giorgi Bogolyubski** from Kiev in southern Russia. They were an ill-matched pair and produced no children, so Tamara—in stark contrast to her father's grisly disposal of unwanted relatives—sent Giorgi into exile. For the next 20 years, Giorgi continued to lead revolts to overthrow her, but each time his efforts failed, Tamara merely sent him back into exile. After her marriage to **David Sosland**—a prince of the Bagrationi line—produced two children, she pursued her goal of restoring Georgia to its former might.

From the year 1200 until her death, Tamara undertook one successful military campaign after another, including a victory at the famous battle of Basiani (1205), where the Turkish sultan surrendered Kars, over which she appointed her son Giorgi governor. After Byzantium was returned to Christianity by the **Fourth Crusade** in 1204, she turned it into a protectorate. She also established numerous other Muslim protectorates and extended her kingdom north beyond the Caucasus Mountains.

Under Tamara's guidance, Georgia experienced a great renaissance of arts and letters, which inspired national poet **Shota Rustaveli** (rōō′stə-vĕ′lē) to write his famous 1600-quatrain epic poem *The Knight in Panther's Skin*. Dedicated to Tamara, it symbolically describes Georgia's glorious era under her rule, calling her "radiant as the rising sun, born to illuminate the world around her... Woman though she is, God had created her to be a sovereign. We may say without flattery that she knows how to rule..."

Queen Tamara.

In 1397, **Margaret** succeeded in uniting the Scandinavian kingdoms of Denmark, Norway and Sweden, a unique accomplishment in the history of the three countries, and the tri-partite union she forged endured for 136 years. A descendent of **Canute (c. 994-1035)**, the first Danish king of England, and the daughter of King **Valdemar IV**, she was married at age 10 to **Haakon VI of Norway (1355-1380)**, the son of **Magnus Eriksson** of Sweden and Norway. Although a year later Haakon lost the Swedish crown, he remained sovereign over Norway, and Margaret, an accomplished scholar, grew up at the Norwegian court.

Margaret's son **Olaf V** was born in 1370. Upon her father's death in 1375, the Danes accepted Olaf as their king, and when Haakon died in 1380 the crown of Norway also passed to him, with Margaret ruling on his behalf. In 1387, Olaf died and she was declared "sovereign lady and ruler" of both countries. To provide a male ruler, in 1389 she adopted her grandnephew, **Eric of Pomerania (Eric III) (1389-1440)**. She then turned her attention to Sweden, where angry nobles had rebelled against their German king, **Albert of Mecklenburg**. After defeating Albert's army, she imprisoned him.

The **Hanseatic League** intervened and ordered Albert released on the condition he pay Margaret 60,000 marks. When he failed to do so, Margaret gained control of Sweden. In June 1397, the three countries were united for the first, and only time in history, under Margaret's control when Eric was crowned king. Even after Eric came of age in 1401, Margaret continued to rule for him. In a commanding but diplomatic way, she moved to consolidate her power and centralize her authority. She did this by setting up a network of provincial sheriffs who governed their own native

Queen Margaret.

territories, a system which served to strengthen allegiance to the crown rather than to a region. She also reformed Danish currency and built up the royal treasury through taxation and by reclamation of hundreds of estates in Denmark and Sweden that had once belonged to the crown.

In foreign affairs, Margaret was a resourceful stateswoman, carefully maintaining her country's neutrality while continuing to recover lost Danish territory. To a large extent she was able to realize her primary goals of creating a unified kingdom and sustaining Scandinavian sovereignty in the face of continued German territorial expansion. Although the tri-partite union ended in 1523, the union between Sweden and Norway continued for over 400 years, until 1814. Margaret died aboard her ship in Flensborg harbor at the age of 59.

15. JOAN OF ARC
1412-1431

Joan of Arc.

The young woman who became a national heroine by decisively turning the tide of the **Hundred Years War (1337-1453)** in France's favor, was the daughter of a Domremy farmer, **Jacques d'Arc,** and his wife **Isabelle de Vouthon**. A pious child, **Joan of Arc** (in French **Jeanne d'Arc**) was 13 when she had her first vision. According to legend, she first heard the voice of God in her father's garden, and over the next five years, saints Catherine, Margaret and Michael the Archangel also appeared to her. At that time, the armies of the English king, **Henry VI (1421-1471)**, occupied all of northern France, including **Rheims**, (rēmz) the traditional site of French coronations. The voices commanded her to liberate Rheims so the dauphin Charles (later **Charles VII, 1403-1461**) could be crowned king.

In 1429, when Joan was 16, the English laid siege to **Orleans**, prompting her to seek an urgent audience with Charles, who met privately with her for two hours. She told him: "I am God's messenger, sent to tell you that you are the true heir to France and the king's son." After her claims were certified by a board of Roman Catholic Church theologians, she was sent to **Tours** to assemble an army. Dressed in a man's white armor, she carried a sword emblazoned with five crosses and a banner with a painting of the king of heaven holding an orb and the motto "Jesus Maria."

After Joan's troops entered Orleans on April 30, they stormed the bastille of Augustines and captured Tourelles. Joan herself planted the first scaling ladder and was wounded in the shoulder. When Charles VII was crowned king on July 14, the **Maid of Orleans** stood proudly by his side. Following other successful routs of the British, Joan was ennobled on December 29 in recognition of what she had done for her country.

The following year, learning that the British had recaptured **Compiegne** in preparation to take Paris, Joan mounted a campaign, but failed and was taken prisoner. The English, hoping to destroy her influence and discredit Charles, turned her over to a Church court in **Rouen** for trial in January 1431. After a 14-month interrogation, she was judged guilty on 12 points that found her visions had been faked, censured her use of masculine dress and, most damning of all, condemned as heresy her belief she was directly responsible to God rather than the Church. On May 30, Joan was burned at the stake in the Old Market Square at Rouen. Gazing intently at a cross she held as the flames engulfed her, she was heard to cry out "Jesus." In 1456, the Church annulled the judgment that had sentenced her to die. In 1920, Joan was canonized by **Pope Benedict XV**. Today, she is honored as the patron saint of France.

The daughter of **Juan II of Castile** and **Isabella of Portugal, Isabella I** was raised near Avila. At age 13, she was brought to the court of her half-brother, King **Henry IV**. Although Henry tried to arrange a marriage for her, she insisted on making her own choice, and in 1469 she wed **Ferdinand of Aragon (1452-1516)**.

When Henry died in 1474, succession to the throne was contested by his daughter, **Juana la Beltraneja (1462-1530)**. On her behalf, **Alfonso V** of Portugal invaded Castile but was defeated in 1479, and Juana withdrew her claim. In the same year, Ferdinand succeeded to the throne of **Aragon**, becoming **Ferdinand II**. Isabella and Ferdinand's union brought the two main Spanish kingdoms together under a joint rule, which laid the foundation for Spain's future greatness as a world power.

Isabella embarked on a reform program to reduce the power of rebellious nobles by resurrecting medieval laws that allowed her to confiscate their lands. She restored the national currency, set up a national police force and army, codified laws and organized courts in large cities. A supporter of education, she founded a new palace school and became a patron for Spanish and Flemish musicians and artists.

Known as the "Catholic Kings," in 1478 Isabella and Ferdinand allowed the Roman Catholic Church to set up the **Inquisition** in Andalusia, opening a dark chapter in Spanish history. Designed as a church tribunal charged with rooting out religious heresy, the Inquisition ultimately expelled over 170,000 Moors (Jews) from Spain. Although Isabella did this to unite Spain under one religion, the expulsion of many of the country's leading intellectuals and scientists proved to be more of a loss than a gain. Isabella and Ferdinand then joined forces to conquer the kingdom of **Granada**, which had been under Muslim rule for several centuries. After a 10-year campaign in which Isabella, traveling with her five children, personally took part by raising funds, Granada fell in 1492 and the Moors were driven from Spain.

In 1492, hoping to secure riches for her country and souls for her church, Isabella gave Italian explorer **Christopher Columbus (1451-1506)** financial support for his venture to find a route to the Orient by sailing west. However, when Columbus returned to Spain with Indians he had taken as slaves, she ordered them freed. Only three days before she died in 1504 at the age of 53, Isabella's last official act was to insist that the natives in the New World be treated fairly.

Isabella and Ferdinand.

17. CATHERINE OF ARAGON
1485-1536

Described by many historians as one of the most beloved queens in English history, **Catherine of Aragon** was the daughter of **Ferdinand II** and **Isabella I** of Spain. She left Spain in 1501 to marry **Arthur**, the eldest son of **Henry VII (1457-1509)**. When Arthur died in 1502, a papal dispensation allowed her to become engaged to his brother, **Henry VIII (1491-1547)**, whom she married after he succeeded his father to the throne in 1509.

For many years, their relationship was a happy one. A woman of considerable education and culture, Catherine was a capable ruler while Henry was absent during the French campaigns (1511- 1514), overseeing Britain's defense against the Scots, who were defeated at the Battle of Flodden in 1513. A great patron of education, she contributed funds for lecturers at the universities at Oxford and Cambridge and financially supported needy scholars. She also enjoyed close friendships with many of the leading intellectuals of the day, including **Sir Thomas More (1478-1535)**, whom Henry later beheaded because of his refusal to sanction his divorce from Catherine.

Because five of six of Catherine's children born between 1510 and 1518 had died with only a female heir—**Mary I (1516-1558)**—surviving, Henry VIII decided to annul his marriage to her so he could remarry. His decision was based on his need to produce a male heir so as to avoid a civil war over succession to the throne. He was also infatuated with the younger and more beautiful **Anne Boleyn** (bŏŏ-lĭn′) **(c. 1507-1536)**. When the Catholic Church refused to grant his petition, Henry broke with Rome and established a new church, the **Church of England**. Fearful of alienating Catherine's nephew **Charles V** of Spain, Pope Clement had delayed his decision on Henry's request for seven years,

Catherine of Aragon.

until 1534. In the meantime, despite death threats and humiliations, Catherine courageously refused to give up her title for that of Princess Dowager and retire to a convent. She also challenged the court hearing that Henry organized in 1529 to declare their marriage invalid on the grounds of consanguinity—the fact she had previously been married to his brother. In 1533, Henry secretly wed Anne Boleyn and convened his own court to grant his request for annulment.

Catherine was then separated from her daughter Mary, whom she never saw again, and held a virtual prisoner on a series of small estates until her death at the age of 51. Despite the hardship of her last years, Catherine fared far better than Anne. After only 1000 days as queen, during which time she produced a female heir (**Elizabeth I**, see page 26), Anne was beheaded in 1536 by her husband so he could marry yet another woman.

Queen of France from 1547 to 1559 and mother of the last three Valois kings, **Catherine de Medici** (də mĕd′ə-chē′) was a major force in French politics for more than 30 years during the prolonged period of religious wars between 1562 and 1598, and was the mastermind of the worst mass killing in French history. She was born in Florence, Italy, the daughter of Florentine ruler **Lorenzo de Medici** (called **Lorenzo the Magnificent**). In a marriage arranged by her uncle, Pope **Clement VII**, at the age of 14 she was wed to the duke of Orleans, who later became King **Henry II** of France. Though she exercised little authority during her husband's reign and that of her eldest son, **Francis II**, who was king for only a year before his death in 1560, she ruled on behalf of her second son, **Charles IX**, until his death in 1574. Catherine devoted most of her energy to preserving the power of her throne. To this end, she tried to maintain a balance between the Huguenots (Protestants), who were led by Admiral **Gaspard de Coligny (1519-1572)**, and the Roman Catholics, whose power was concentrated in the house of Guise. A Catholic herself, Catherine did not want the Huguenots to get the upper hand, nor did she wish to see them crushed, as they served as an effective counterbalance to limit the power of the Guise family. Her policies proved unsuccessful, and a series of religious civil wars erupted in 1562.

Her political aspirations also affected her family's personal lives. In 1560 she arranged for her daughter **Elizabeth of Valois (1545-1568)** to become the third wife of Spain's Catholic king, **Philip II (1527-1598)**. She also found it advantageous to have another daughter, **Margaret of Valois (1553-1615)**, marry the Protestant Henry of Navarre, later **Henry IV (1589-1610)** of France. However, Catherine had become worried about the growing influence that Huguenot leader Coligny exerted upon her son Charles.

After an assassination attempt on Coligny failed, Catherine planned an attack on prominent Huguenot leaders when they gathered in Paris for her daughter's wedding on August 24, 1572. The carnage began at dawn, and over the next two days 20,000 Huguenots, including Coligny, were murdered in what would come to be known as the **St. Bartholomew's Day Massacre**. The mass killings continued across France, with the final death toll estimated at 50,000.

Catherine's power declined somewhat after her third son, **Henry III (1574-1589)**, ascended the throne, and she died in Blois, France, shortly before Henry was assassinated, ending the Valois line.

The St. Bartholomew's Day Massacre of 1572.

The 45-year reign of the charismatic and popular queen **Elizabeth I** ushered in era of national achievement and economic prosperity which established England as an international power. She was born in Greenwich, the daughter of **Henry VIII (1491-1547)** and his second wife, **Anne Boleyn (1507-1536)**. After her mother was executed and her parents' marriage invalidated so her father could remarry, she was declared illegitimate. In 1544, her succession was restored by Parliament behind her half-siblings **Edward (1537-1553)** and **Mary I (1516-1558)**.

When she became queen in 1558, Elizabeth moved to settle religious unrest. She reverted to Protestantism and had Parliament pass laws that formed the doctrinal basis for the Church of England which, by the **Elizabethan Compromise (1559)**, became England's official church. She supported the Protestant cause in Scotland, and when her Roman Catholic cousin **Mary, Queen of Scots (1542-1587)** sought refuge in England after being forced to abdicate, Elizabeth faced one of her most delicate political crises. Since Mary was next in line of succession, Catholic nobles considered her the rightful English heir and plotted to usurp the throne, which forced Elizabeth to first imprison, then execute Mary in 1587.

Elizabeth instituted currency reforms, employment laws and measures providing relief for the poor. She also showed a characteristic shrewdness of judgment when she appointed **Sir William Cecil (1563-1612)** her chief secretary. A practical thinker like Elizabeth, he advised her to maintain a balance of power with France and Spain. Thus for her entire life, despite Parliamentary pressure, Elizabeth continued to refuse all offers of marriage, declaring herself to be the **Virgin Queen**.

Elizabeth's domination of the era that bears her name was due in great part to the reawakening of nationalistic fervor that she inspired. With peace, England was able to turn its energies to developing its industries and strengthening its economy. Through the exploits of adventurers such as **Sir Francis Drake (c. 1540-1596)**, it increased its colonial holdings and became a great maritime power, which in 1588 was able to defeat the **Spanish Armada**. A new currency was introduced that stabilized prices and restored confidence in English currency. Literature and arts flourished, producing some of England's most renowned writers, such as **William Shakespeare (1564-1616)**.

Elizabeth died in London at the age of 70. Today, she is still considered to be one of the greatest rulers in the history of England.

Elizabeth I.

20. QUEEN JINGA (JINGA MBANDI)
c. 1580-1663

In the **Ndongo** tribe she was called **Jinga Mbandi**, but the name given to her by the Portuguese and in popular use today in the **People's Republic of Angola** is **Queen Jinga**. A true warrior queen, she united the people of Ndongo, **Matamba, Congo, Casnje, Dembos, Kissama** and the **Central Planalto** and succeeded in creating the greatest alliance of tribes ever formed to fight against the forces of foreign colonization in Angola. Daughter of a Ndongo **ngola** (king), Jinga lived in central West Africa, where Christian missionaries arrived in 1483. Later came Portuguese traders who were primarily interested in supplying slaves to Brazilian plantations and mines. In 1576, the Portuguese extended their influence to the city of Luanda and Portugal appointed governors to enforce colonial law. Thus began a century of war which, although ultimately won by the Portuguese, made Jinga a national heroine.

Queen Jinga.

In return for a guarantee of autonomy, tribal chiefs often sold members of rival tribes to slave traders. When the Portuguese exiled her brother for demanding total self-rule, Jinga skillfully negotiated his release. She even agreed to be baptized, taking the name **Anna de Sousa** in honor of the incoming governor.

In 1624, when her brother died and she became queen, Jinga resumed her tribal religion. The Portuguese, seeking to replace her with a ruler more loyal to their cause, declared war on her. She immediately made an alliance with the Casnje, effectively closing off all slave routes. In 1630, she allied herself with the fierce, cannibalistic **Jagas** of Matamba and gained their respect as a strong leader by participating in many of their traditional rituals dressed in men's clothing.

After forging a pan-African alliance of tribes, Jinga began leading raids against the Portuguese, freeing many Africans destined for lives of servitude in the New World. In 1641, she drew the Portuguese troops so far inland in pursuit that Luanda was seized by the Dutch. However, after victories in 1643, 1647 and 1648, she was forced to sign a peace treaty in 1654 in order to free her sister **Mukumbu**, whom the Portuguese held captive.

Nearly 200 years later, American abolitionists cited Jinga's bravery and intelligence to disprove arguments that African-American slaves were not the equal of whites. Immediately after Angola won its independence from Portugal on November 11, 1975, the new government named a street after Jinga in downtown Luanda. Contemporary Angolan textbooks praise her heroic career: "Even if she was not successful then, her great dream did not disappear. Her idea of a union of the Angolan people in its struggle against colonialism is today realized."

Pocahontas (pō-kə-hoŏn'təs), whose Indian name **Matoaka** means "playful," was the youngest daughter of **Powhatan (c. 1550-1618)**, chief of the Algonquin confederacy of Indian tribes in the tidewater region of Virginia. By her marriage to one of the colonists, she played a key role in helping **Jamestown**, the first permanent English colony in America, flourish during its early years.

Located on an island in the James River southeast of present-day Richmond, Jamestown was first settled in 1607 by a group led by investors of the **London Company**, one of whom was **John Smith (1579-1631)**. As one story tells it, on one of his expeditions to map the surrounding area, Smith was taken captive by warriors from Chief Powhatan's tribe but was saved from being clubbed to death when 12-year-old Pocahontas interceded. After this, Pocahontas helped to establish trade between her tribe and the settlers. This story first appeared in Smith's *Generall Historie of Virginia* (1624) and was later romanticized in an eighteenth-century novel entitled *Captain Smith and Princess Pocahontas* (1805).

Whether the Smith incident happened or not, the fact is that relations between the Indians and the settlers later deteriorated. In 1612, Pocahontas was taken hostage by Captain **Samuel Argall** and held in exchange for English prisoners and materials seized by the Indians. During this time, at her request, she learned the English language and was baptized a Christian, taking the name **Rebecca**. She also met **John Rolfe (1585-1622)**, a planter 10 years her senior who had come to the colony in 1610. Rolfe is credited with introducing the cultivation of the **tobacco plant** into America.

Upon her marriage to Rolfe in 1614, Pocahontas' father gave the couple land and their union ushered in eight years of peace for the Jamestown colony. In 1616, Rolfe took his wife to England, where she was presented at court to King **James I (1556-1625)**. Dressed in ladylike finery and able to speak English, Pocahontas was proof that the New World could indeed be "civilized" and made a hospitable place for settlers.

On the eve of her return home, Pocahontas died of smallpox and was buried in the chapel of the parish church in Gravesend, England. John Rolfe returned to America, where he became a member of Virginia's first Council of State. Today, many prominent Virginians claim descent from his and Pocahontas' son, **Thomas Rolfe**.

Pocahontas saved John Smith from execution.

22. MARY WORTLEY MONTAGU
1689-1762

Lady Mary Montagu, the pioneer of smallpox inoculation in Europe, was a prodigious writer of letters, diaries and poetry. Born in London, England, the eldest child of **Evelyn Pierrepont, duke of Kingston**, she educated herself by using her father's library. In 1712, in order to avoid an arranged marriage, she eloped with **Edward Montagu (d. 1763)**, who later served as the English Ambassador at Constantinople, Turkey, from 1716 to 1718.

Outspoken and forceful, Montagu's writings are considered to be among the most important literary documents of eighteenth century England. Her ongoing feud with satirist **Alexander Pope (1688-1744)** only added to her notoriety. While living in Turkey, she wrote letters chronicling her life in the Middle East, which were published after her death in 1763. She also wrote a volume of poetry, *Town Eclogues* (1747). In 1803, her Turkish letters and other writings about English life and her travels on the continent were collected in *Works*.

During Montagu's lifetime, smallpox killed 45,000 people annually in Great Britain alone. In Turkey she observed the procedure of **variolation**, whereby fluids from the victim of an attack were inserted with a needle into the veins of another person. Certain that such a procedure could guard against smallpox, upon her return to England she had her daughter inoculated. She also interested **Caroline, Princess of Wales** in the procedure, and under Mary's direction, experiments were carried out on condemned prisoners. After these tests proved successful, the practice of inoculation spread rapidly throughout Britain, despite opposition from the medical profession. To counter these attacks, Montagu anonymously published a tract entitled *Plain Account of the Inoculating of the Smallpox by a Turkey Merchant.*

By proving her theory that inoculation with mild smallpox could provide immunity from a serious case, Mary Montagu paved the way for public acceptance of inoculation in Europe. Her early work on variolation constituted the first step toward the discovery of the theory that germs cause disease.

In failing health and at the behest of her daughter Mary, countess of Bute, whose husband was then Prime Minister, Mary Montagu returned to London, where she died in August 1762.

Mary Wortley Montagu.

29

23. EMILIE DU CHATELET
1706-1749

Gabrielle-Emilie le Tonnelier de Breteuil, a mathematician and Newtonian scientist, was born in France, the daughter of the **Baron of Preuilly**, chief of protocol at the French court. Because Emilie at five feet nine inches was taller than most male contemporaries (she was a head taller than the philosopher Voltaire), her parents were convinced she would never marry, and so they provided her with the best education possible.

At 19, Emilie married the **Marquis Florent Claude du Chatelet-Lomont**. Her social position enabled her to hire the greatest scientists of the time to tutor her in

Emilie du Chatelet.

advanced physics and mathematics. With the rise of Paris cafe society in the 1730s, Chatelet—disguised as a man because the only women allowed in such establishments were courtesans—was able to penetrate the male-only scientific network.

After meeting the philosopher **Voltaire (1694-1778)** in 1733, the two remodeled one of her husband's run-down estates at Cirey by transforming its great hall into a fully-equipped laboratory. Chatelet conducted experiments on **Issac Newton's (1642-1727)** optics and her laboratory became a center for Newtonian science. She is credited with influencing Voltaire to change his focus from writing plays to studying physics and metaphysics. In 1736, they collaborated on *Elements de la Philosophie de Newton*, a popular account of Newton's theories.

Believing that Newton's purely scientific, materialistic philosophy did not offer a complete explanation and that scientific theory demanded a foundation in metaphysics, Chatelet incorporated theories of natural philosophy by **Gottfried Leibniz** (līb′nĭts) **(1646-1716)** in her *Institutions de Physique*, an updated introductory physics text for her son. Following its publication in 1740, younger scientists began to arrive at Cirey to study with her.

The culmination of Chatelet's scientific work was her two-volume translation of Newton's *Principia*, which also included her commentaries, the first part of which was strictly mathematical and the second part a six-chapter, greatly improved revision of *Elements*. After its publication in 1759, Newton's scientific method became an established part of the **French Enlightenment**. Even today, her work remains the only French translation of Newton's book. A few days after giving birth to a daughter at Luneville in September, she died of an infection at the age of 43.

24. CATHERINE THE GREAT
1729-1796

As empress of Russia (1762-1796), the gifted and ambitious **Catherine the Great** continued the work of westernization and expansion begun by **Peter the Great** and helped shape the modern state of Russia. Born **Sophie Fredericke Auguste von Anhalt-Zerbst** in Stettin (now Szczecin) Poland, she was wed to Grand Duke **Peter of Holstein (Peter III, 1728-1762)** in 1745. Within months of succeeding to the throne, the disagreeable and unstable Peter had aroused so much resentment that his palace guards overthrew him and placed Catherine on the throne. Rather than rule for her seven-year-old son Paul (later **Paul I, 1754-1801**) she declared herself queen in July 1762.

Influenced by reading works of the **Enlightenment**, Catherine was determined to make Russian society as cultured as that of Paris or Berlin. She corresponded with a number of French writers, including **Voltaire (1694-1778)**, and employed experts to collect art and antiquities. Under her direction, St. Petersburg became one of the cultural centers of Europe. She also strengthened Russia's economy by abolishing trade restrictions and promoted the development of underpopulated areas by encouraging settlement.

Although Catherine attempted to apply the ideas of the Enlightenment to domestic reform, most of her new laws were designed to win support from the nobles. She exempted them from military service and expanded their rights over serfs, a system frequently used by rulers in Europe prior to the **French Revolution (1789-1799)** which has since been called **benevolent despotism**. As a result, peasant unrest grew, culminating in a massive peasant revolt in 1773, which was crushed by military force.

To revise the **Code of Laws of 1649**, for two years Catherine worked on an *Instruction*, which would provide equal protection

Catherine the Great.

under the law and pursue crime prevention rather than harsh punishment—a system far ahead of its time. In 1767, She convened a Legislative Commission to encode it into law. Unfortunately, commission members became bogged down in self-interests and a year later she disbanded it. However, her 1775 reorganization of provincial administrations did prove successful. She also founded a medical college and the first Russian schools for girls.

Catherine's foreign policy was aimed at expanding Russian holdings, and judged in this context, it was a success. As a result of two wars with Turkey (1768-1774 and 1787-1791), she gained control of the Crimea and access to the Black Sea and the Dardanelles Strait. By taking part with Prussia and Austria in the three partitions of Poland (1772, 1793, 1795), she annexed a vast amount of territory on Russia's western border.

25. CAROLINE HERSCHEL
1750-1848

Caroline Herschel (hûr′shəl) was one of the most famous and admired women astronomers in history, and her work helped to open the field of astronomy to other women. Born into a large family of musicians in Hanover, Germany, she went to England at 22 to train as a singer and assume the role of housekeeper to her brother, the astronomer **William Herschel (1738-1822)**. After discovering the planet Uranus in 1781, William was appointed King's Astronomer and Caroline became his assistant.

While other astronomers had to confine their observations to closer objects such as the planets, William's continual improvements in the magnification capabilities of his telescopes enabled him to identify distant stars. Often scanning the heavens through the night and spending their days making calculations, William and Caroline jointly founded **Sidereal** (sī-dêr′ĕ-əl) **Astronomy**—the study of stars—and advanced astronomy from a science of the solar system to a science of stellar systems. Between 1783 and 1802, they documented 2500 new nebulae and star clusters. Eventually, they also discovered 1000 double stars.

During independent observations in 1783, Caroline discovered three nebulae, and in August 1786 she became the first woman to discover a comet. Over the next 11 years, she found 10 more comets. In 1787, the king granted both Herschels additional funds for their work, which marked the first time a woman had been appointed as an official assistant to the court astronomer.

In 1797, Caroline completed the *Catalogue of 860 Stars Observed by Flamsteed*, as well as a catalogue of 561 stars which had accidentally been omitted from the *British Catalogue*. Both were published by the **Royal Astronomical Society** in 1798.

Caroline Herschel is one of the most important women in the history of astronomy. She was the first woman to discover a comet.

At the age of 75, she completed a formidable work on the positions of some 2500 nebulae entitled *A Catalogue of the Nebulae Which Have Been Observed by William Herschel in a Series of Sweeps*, for which she received the **Gold Medal** of the Royal Astronomical Society in 1828. In 1835, the Society voted unanimously to bestow honorary membership on the two leading women scientists of the early nineteenth century: Caroline Herschel and **Mary Fairfax Somerville** (see page 38). After William's death in 1822, Caroline returned to Hanover, where she lived until her own death at age 97.

Although **Eli Whitney (1765-1825)** is generally given sole credit for the invention of the **cotton gin**, a machine that revolutionized farming in the southern United States and profoundly affected the history of the region, his friend and benefactress, **Catherine Littlefield Greene** was actually a co-inventor. The daughter of a prominent Rhode Island family, she married American Revolutionary War General **Nathanial Greene (1742-1786)**. Soon after the Greenes and their five children moved to **Mulberry Grove**, a plantation on Georgia's Savannah River, Nathanial died.

During a vacation in 1792, Greene met Whitney, who was traveling south to become a tutor. When this job fell through, she invited him to stay at her home. Whitney, who loved to work with his hands, soon displayed exceptional mechanical talent. He devised a new part for Greene's embroidery frame and built toys for her children.

During a gathering at Greene's plantation, a group of local planters discussed the future of agriculture in the South and agreed the crop of choice was cotton. However, removing cotton seeds was such tedious work, it took one person an entire day to produce a cleaned pound. Greene told the planters to talk to Whitney about their problem.

For the next several weeks, Whitney worked on the design and construction of the cotton gin, a machine consisting of a wooden cylinder encircled by a row of slender spikes. However, his initial model was significantly flawed. Although it could pull the seeds from the cotton, the loose seeds clogged the roller. When he talked to Greene about his dilemma, she recommended that he install a brush and gave him one from her kitchen. Once installed, the revolving brush successfully cleaned the spikes, pushing the seeds into a separate compartment. The gin, which was cranked by hand, was capable of cleaning up to 50 pounds of cotton a day.

Whitney went into partnership with Greene's plantation manager, **Phineas Miller (d. 1803)**, whom Greene married in 1796. Although the men received a patent, they were unable to meet the demand for the machines and country blacksmiths began to pirate their simple design. During the ensuing lengthy and costly patent fight, it was Greene who provided the funds for the men to stay in business, eventually selling her plantation in 1800 to pay lawsuits costs. Whitney finally won full title to the cotton gin in 1807. However, neither he nor Greene ever realized much profit from their invention which had turned cotton into the most important cash crop in the South.

The cotton gin.

When **Marie Anne Pierette Paulze** was 14, her father arranged a marriage with **Antoine Lavoisier** (lə-vwä′zē-ā′) **(1743-1794)**, a man twice her age who was already an established chemist. For the next 25 years, the Lavoisiers collaborated continuously. Their work on heat and fire brought about a fundamental transition in the science of chemistry by replacing the old beliefs of **alchemy** with a new system of scientific principles, thus laying the groundwork for modern chemistry.

Marie first learned Latin and English so she could translate chemical studies. Her translations, with original commentaries, titled *Annales de Chimie*, were published in 1792. She also illustrated her husband's numerous publications, assisted with experiments, took all the notes, kept laboratory records and maintained their scientific correspondence.

Completing some of the earliest known quantitative experiments, the Lavoisiers were able to demonstrate that burning is a process that involves the combination of a substance with a portion of the atmosphere—an element Antoine later named **oxygen**. These findings are described in *Methode de Nomenclature Chimique*, the first modern chemistry text. In it, the term **element** is redefined as being a simple substance that cannot be broken down by any known method of chemical analysis. Marie's copperplate illustrations, original drawings and watercolors for this book survive as the most famous of her works.

Marie and her husband also discovered the **Law of Conservation of Matter**, which states that the weight of the products from a chemical reaction must equal the weight of the reagents. Their studies of animal metabolism demonstrated the role of oxygen in animal and plant respiration.

After both her husband and father were guillotined in 1794 during the **French Revolution (1789-1799),** Marie completed *Memoires de Chimie*, an eight-volume work, and published it under her husband's name in 1805. Marie Lavoisier spent the last years of her life as a successful businesswoman and philanthropist, but found it increasingly difficult to continue her scientific work alone. She died in 1836 at the age of 78.

Marie Lavoisier.

Considered by historians as the first modern feminist, **Mary Wollstonecraft** (wŏŏl'stŏn-krăft) was born in England during the Age of Reason, a period of revolution and change in America and France. Her childhood was unhappy and marked by abuse, and she left home at 21 to earn her own living as a teacher and governess.

Following the modest success of her first book, a novel entitled *Mary, A Fiction* (1788), she moved to London and supported herself as a writer, reader and translator. There she became involved with a radical circle of intellectuals with whom she dined each Thursday—revolutionary **Thomas Paine (1737-1809)**, poet **William Blake (1757-1827)** and chemist **Joseph Priestly (1733-1804)**, among others. Shunning the traditional restraints that normally bound women, she soon made a name for herself by actively defending the most progressive ideas of her day. Her pioneer work, *A Vindication of the Rights of Women* (1792), which was based on the premise that freedom and equality apply to women as well as men, caused an immediate sensation and made her one of the most famous—and controversial—women in Europe. Wollstonecraft also insisted that governments were obliged to provide an education for all their citizens, with equal access guaranteed for women, arguing that if a woman "be not prepared by education to become the companion of man, she will stop the progress of knowledge."

Wollstonecraft also asserted that a marriage where the wife was a mere adornment, a bearer of children or used only for physical release was unacceptable and proposed there be intellectual companionship and equality between partners. These crusading ideas would not be repeated, much less acted upon, for over a 100 years.

In 1797, she married her second husband, political philosopher **William God-**

Mary Wollstonecraft.

win (1756-1836). That same year she gave birth to their daughter, Mary (later **Mary Shelley (1797-1851)**, author of the famous horror story, *Frankenstein*), and died soon after of an infection.

Wollstonecraft's other works include *Original Stories from Real Life* (1791) and *A Vindication of the Rights of Man* (1793). Her letters were published in *Memoirs of the Author of the Rights of Women* (1798). For an excellent novelization of her life and times, see Frances Sherwood's *Vindication* (1993).

After the fall of the **Bastille** (bă-stĕl′) in 1789 during the **French Revolution (1789-1799)**, the streets of Paris became a chaotic, dangerous place, so 13-year-old **Marie-Sophie Germain's** parents confined her to home. Seeking refuge in her father's extensive library, she came upon the story of the death of **Archimedes** (är′kə-mē′dēz) **(287-212 BC)**. The Greek mathematician, completely absorbed in his study of a geometric figure in the sand, failed to respond to an invading Roman soldier's questions and was speared to death. Inspired, Germain decided to learn all she could about what had so fascinated Archimedes—mathematics.

Germain's parents, however, were concerned that such "brainwork" was not healthy for a girl and actively tried to discourage her. Undeterred, Germain often studied through the night, teaching herself differential calculus. In 1795, denied admittance at the newly opened Ecole Polytechnique because she was a woman, she obtained lecture notes on chemistry and from an analysis class taught by **Joseph Lagrange (1736-1814)**. She then submitted a paper to Lagrange under the pseudonym "LeBlanc." Lagrange was so impressed with the paper that, after learning who the author was, he went to Germain's home to congratulate her. Thus encouraged, Germain began to correspond with several scholars and scientists. She was particularly interested in the number theory of **Carl Gauss (1777-1855)**, and for three years she exchanged letters with him using the name "Monsieur LeBlanc." When the French army invaded his German hometown, she asked the commanding general—an old family friend—to spare Gauss' life. When Gauss learned Germain's true identity, he was even more favorably impressed and shared her work with his colleagues.

Sophie Germain.

After physicist **Ernest Chladni** demonstrated how patterns could be reproduced by sprinkling sand on a plate and striking the plate with a violin bow, interest in the resonant vibration of elastic bodies was renewed. The French Academy called for papers that would explain and predict the unusual patterns that sand or powder make on reverberating flexible surfaces. In 1816, Germain won the Academy's grand prize for her mathematical formula on the **Law of Vibrating Elastic Surfaces**. Her formula was subsequently used by scientists to solve practical problems in building construction, making the building of structures, such as the **Eiffel Tower**, possible. Sophie Germain spent the remainder of life independently working on number theory. She died in Paris of cancer at the age of 55.

Devout Society of Friends (Quaker) minister and prison reformer **Elizabeth Gurney** was born in Norfolk, England, the fourth of 12 children of a prosperous banker. The Gurneys were "wide" Quakers, meaning that the women did not wear the traditional gray dress and bonnet nor the men a wide-brimmed hat.

A turning point in Elizabeth's life occurred when, at the age of 18, she met American evangelist **William Savery** after he spoke at a Norwich religious revival meeting. Following this, she became a "plain" Friend, adopting their gray costume and becoming more orthodox.

In 1800, Elizabeth married **John Fry**, a London merchant, and in 1809, she became a Quaker minister. She had already borne eight of her 10 children when she first visited **Newgate Prison** in 1813 at the urging of a clergyman from America who had gone to Newgate to work with the inmates. Appalled at the squalid living conditions of the prisoners, especially the women, he had sought Fry's assistance. She later said that at Newgate she had found "half naked women, struggling together ... with the most boisterous violence... I felt as if I were going into a den of wild beasts."

Known as an effective public speaker, Fry often read the Bible aloud to an overflowing room of women. Said a fellow minister who witnessed one of these sessions: "There they sat in respectful silence, every eye fixed upon ... the gentle lady ... never till then, and never since then, have I heard any one read as Elizabeth Fry read..."

Besides her ministerial duties, Fry also began an aggressive campaign for more humane treatment of women prisoners and of convicts who were transported to New South Wales, Australia, which at that time was being used as a British penal colony. She sought to keep men separate from women, to seek employment for prisoners, and to classify and segregate the more violent ones from the weaker ones. She also founded a prison school and a **Prisoners Aid Society** in 1817.

After giving compelling testimony to the 1818 Royal Commission, Fry toured the British isles in the 1820s, inspecting facilities and outlining improvements, and founding women's associations and prison reform groups. Having become famous throughout Britain, she traveled through Europe to meet with heads of state. In 1838, King **Louis Phillipe (1773-1850)** (called the **Citizen King**), invited her to France to examine French prisons. Her report led to penal reforms there. During her lifetime, Fry also worked to raise the standards, training and status of nurses, to improve educational facilities for women and to secure housing and employment for London's poor.

Elizabeth Fry.

31. MARY FAIRFAX SOMERVILLE
1780-1872

Upon her death in 1872, *The London Post* acclaimed her as **The Queen of Nineteenth Century Science**. A heroine in both scientific and activist circles, **Mary Fairfax Somerville** was an outspoken supporter of women's suffrage and the first to sign a petition for women's rights presented to Parliament by **John Stuart Mill (1806-1873)**. Her enduring scientific legacy and widespread popularity was due to her ability to explain the prevailing state of science in terms educated laymen could readily understand.

The only daughter of a Scottish admiral, Somerville grew up in the seacoast village of Burtisland. Although her formal education consisted of one year at boarding school, her uncle inspired her with stories of women scholars of the ancient world. She also studied *Elements* by **Euclid (c. 3rd-2nd century BC)** and an algebra text she obtained from her brother's tutor. Soon she was reading *Principles* by **Sir Issac Newton (1642-1727)**, and went on to study botany, meteorology, astronomy, higher mathematics and physics.

After publishing several scientific papers, her translation of *Mecanique Celeste* by **Pierre Laplace (1749-1827)**, which was entitled *Mechanism of the Heavens*, appeared in 1831. *Preliminary Dissertation*, her addition to the original text, outlined the basic mathematics a reader needed to understand Laplace's concepts, a history of the subject and her explanation of the book, accompanied by original drawings, diagrams and mathematical calculations. *Mechanism* remained a standard text in higher mathematics and astronomy for the rest of the century. In her book *Physical Sciences* (1834), Somerville "tried to make the laws by which the material world is governed more familiar to my countrywomen." *Sciences* went through 10 editions in the next 40 years and was trans-

Mary Fairfax Somerville.

lated into several languages. It proved to be a popular book, both with scientists and the general public.

In 1838, Somerville published her most successful book, *Physical Geography*. It was a purely descriptive work and contained many of her political views, such as her stance against slavery. Honorary memberships in the Britain's Royal Astronomical Society and the societies of numerous other European countries were offered to her. Her last book, *On Molecular and Microscopic Science*, published in 1869 when she was 89, covered topics ranging from atomic theory to a catalogue of plants.

Mary Somerville died peacefully in her sleep at the age of 92 in Naples, Italy.

Born among the **Lembi Shoshone** Indian tribe of western Montana, **Sacajawea** (săk′ə-jə-wē′ə) was kidnapped as a teenager by the **Hadatsa** Indians, who took her to their village on the upper Missouri in North Dakota. In 1804, she was purchased by French Canadian trader **Toussaint Charbonneau** and she became one of his two Indian wives.

The expedition led by **Meriwether Lewis (1774-1809)** and **William Clark (1770-1838)** traveled up the Missouri River from St. Louis, Missouri, in May 1804, and during a stopover at a Mandan village in South Dakota, they hired Charbonneau as an interpreter. He brought Sacajawea, who spoke Shoshone and Siouan. Shortly before the expedition set out from Fort Mandan in April 1805, she gave birth to a son, **Jean-Baptiste**. Known as "Pomp," or "Pompey," he made the 8000-mile journey in a cradleboard strapped to his mother's back.

As the sole female member of the 40-man group, Sacajawea proved invaluable. Not only did she provide expert guidance through the wilderness of Montana, but her presence was viewed as a token of peace, and she was able to communicate with the tribes they encountered through language and signs. She also introduced the use of wild plants as food and she saved the expedition's journals after her husband accidentally capsized a canoe. Members of the expedition later praised her "resourcefulness, courage and good humor," but said her husband had "mistreated her and was not worthy of his hire." For his services, Charbonneau was paid $503.33. Sacajawea received nothing.

In August 1805, in the three forks region of the Missouri in present-day Montana, Sacajawea was reunited with her brother, the tribal chief. At her request, her brother **Cameahwait** provided horses, supplies and guides for them to use in their crossing of the Rocky Mountains. The expedition continued up the Clearwater, Snake and Columbia Rivers, reaching the Pacific Ocean in November 1805. On the return journey, Sacajawea accompanied Clark's party down the Yellowstone River, disembarking with her family at the mouth of the Knife River while the expedition returned to St. Louis, Missouri, in 1806.

The remainder of Sacajawea's life is uncertain. It is believed that she and her husband visited St. Louis sometime after 1806, leaving their son with Clark, who sponsored his education. One story says she died of disease in 1812, but another story reports she lived to be 100 years old. In addition to numerous memorials along the explorers' route, Sacajawea also has a river, a mountain and a pass named in her honor.

Sacajawea.

After crowning himself king of France in 1804, **Napoleon Bonaparte (1769-1821)** embarked on a campaign of conquest between 1806 and 1814. Following victories against Austria (1805) and Prussia (1806), he set out to force England into submission by cutting off its trade. To this end, he undertook the **Peninsular War (1808-1814)** in Spain and Portugal. It was during this campaign that 18-year-old **La Saragossa**, also known as the **Maid of Saragossa**, became a national heroine when she valiantly rallied her countrymen during the first French siege of Saragossa (in Spanish, Zaragoza) in Spain, between June 15 and August 15, 1808. In 1807, Napoleon forced Spain's King **Charles IV (1788-1808)** to agree to let his troops pass through Spain to attack Portugal and to provide Spanish troops to assist him. In return, he promised to divide a conquered Portugal between France and Spain. Once French troops reached Portugal's capital at Lisbon, however, Napoleon turned against Spain, and by March 1808 he had seized the capital at Madrid.

The Spanish, realizing Napoleon's treachery, rose in revolt. Over 100,000 men were gathered. They were brave and enthusiastic but lacked arms, organization and commanders. Napoleon immediately counterattacked. His key targets became the ports on Spain's east coast and the fortress of Saragossa, a provincial capital located on the Ebro River. In the heat of the French attack, La Saragossa arrived at the Portillo gate with food for the soldiers but found that many were either dead or had abandoned their positions. Picking up a match from the hand of a dead gunner, she declared that she would not leave until the battle had been won, then lit the fuse on the 620-pound cannon. Inspired by her show of bravery, the remaining soldiers returned to combat.

True to her word, Saragossa remained at the forefront of the fighting until the French retreated two months later. In the interim, she displayed incredible bravery by rescuing the wounded under fire and tending to their injuries without rest. One romanticized story describes how, in the thick of battle "an unknown maiden issued from the Church of Nostra Donna de Pillas ... in white raiment, a cross suspended from her neck ... her eyes sparkling with supernatural luster."

Thanks in part to Saragossa's leadership, the Spanish forces successfully repelled the French. Saragossa became a symbol of national pride, liberty and heroism and was immortalized by the poet **Lord Byron (1788-1824)** in *Childe Harold* and in paintings by **Goya (1746-1828)**.

The worst of the French siege of Saragossa was at the Portillo gate.

34. LUCRETIA COFFIN MOTT
1793-1880

Born on Nantucket Island, Massachusetts, **Lucretia Coffin** was educated at Nine Partners, a Society of Friends (Quaker) boarding school in Poughkeepsie, New York. When she learned that the men teachers at her school were paid twice as much as the women, she decided to become a women's rights activist. At 18, she married **James Mott (1788-1868)**, who had been one of her teachers and shared her views.

After 1817, Mott became prominent in the Quakers and when in 1827 the sect split into two factions, she and her husband joined the **Hicksites**—the liberal faction led by **Elias Hicks**. In 1833, the Motts helped found the **American Antislavery Society** and in 1840 they were delegates to an international antislavery convention in London. Lucretia and **Elizabeth Cady Stanton** (see page 48), who also attended the convention, were excluded from participation by being seated behind a heavy curtain, so all they could do was merely listen to the proceedings. Angered by this discriminatory treatment, both women vowed to devote their energies solely to the cause of equal rights for women.

In 1848, Mott and Stanton called the first **Women's Rights Convention** to "discuss the social, civil and religious condition and rights of women." The convention, which was held at a Wesleyan chapel in Seneca Falls, New York, drew more than 100 people, both male and female. The delegates agreed that their primary goal was universal suffrage for women and they adopted Stanton's *Declaration of Sentiments*, which was patterned on the **Declaration of Independence**. This statement was the first public demand for women's voting rights. After the convention, although many prominent Americans supported the new movement, others branded the suffragists as "unfeminine"

Lucretia Coffin Mott.

and accused them of immorality. At times when suffragist leaders undertook speaking tours, they were subjected to physical violence.

Following the passage of the second **Fugitive Slave Law** in 1850, the Motts' made their home a station on **Harriet Tubman's Underground Railroad** (see page 54), an organization that helped slaves flee to freedom. In 1866, Lucretia was named the first president of the **American Equal Rights Association**. For many years, both of the Motts traveled widely, lecturing on women's suffrage, temperance and world peace. When her husband died in 1868, she took his place as president of the **Pennsylvania Peace Society**. Lucretia Mott died at Roadside, her home north of Philadelphia, at the age of 87.

35. CATHERINE BEECHER
1800-1878

Many of the ideas about American education considered "modern" today actually originated with **Catherine Beecher**, a pioneer in mathematics education and education for women. She was born in the state of New York in 1800, one of 13 children of Presbyterian minister **Lyman Beecher (1775-1863)** and a mother who loved to solve mathematical problems. Her famous siblings include **Harriet Beecher Stowe** (see page 44), and abolitionist **Henry Ward Beecher (1813-1887)**.

At a time when there was no university education for women, at age 20, Beecher undertook a two-year independent study course to prepare herself for teaching. She later opened the **Hartford Seminary for Girls** in Hartford, Connecticut, where her sister Harriet was first a pupil and then a teacher.

In 1832, Beecher opened the **Western Female Institute** in Cincinnati to train teachers for the vast territory of the West, and through this school and other organizations she set up around the country, 30,000 teachers received training. In addition to expanding the school curriculum to include physical education classes, she was one of the first to teach home economics as a school subject. She wrote several books on "domestic science," including *Treatise on Domestic Economy* which explained how to systematize homemaking skills. In 1832, she became one of the first American women to write a mathematics textbook, *Arithmetic Simplified*. Her work also led her to found the **American Women's Educational Association**.

Some of Catherine Beecher's innovative ideas included: (1) dividing students below college level into smaller classes that were approximately equal in ability; (2) using the most gifted students to assist her in class; (3) limiting mathematics class size to six to 10 students, as she believed this was

Catherine Beecher.

the maximum a teacher could teach effectively; (4) having teachers teach only two or three subjects instead of all subjects; (5) encouraging teachers to use "objects of sight" (visual aids) in mathematics instruction; (6) using blackboards to work problems—rather than having students memorize everything, as was then the custom—and placing the boards all around the room, which was a very advanced idea at that time; and (7) expecting students not merely to calculate the answers by rote but to fully understand what they were doing and be able to communicate their reasoning in mathematical language.

36. DOROTHEA DIX
1802-1887

Born in Hampden, Maine, the daughter of an itinerant preacher, pioneer prison reformer **Dorothea Dix** described her poverty-stricken childhood as a "time of loneliness and despair." At 12, she ran away from home and persuaded her grandmother in Boston to take her in. For 15 years, she operated schools both in her grandmother's and in her aunt's homes. She also wrote several children's books, including *Conversations on Common Things*, which reached its 60th edition by 1869.

The turning point in Dix's life occurred when she volunteered to teach a Sunday school class in an East Cambridge jail, where she was horrified to discover that mentally ill people were being kept in unheated cells, even in the most frigid weather. The jailer explained to Dix that insane people didn't feel changes in temperature and refused to honor her pleas to provide heat. Dix then took the case to court—and won.

Over the next two years, Dix visited jails, workhouses, almshouses and hospitals all over Massachusetts, documenting their appalling conditions. In 1845, **Samuel Howe** presented her *Memorial to the Massachusetts Legislature*, in which Dix called their attention to the the "present state of insane persons confined ... in cages, closets, cellars, pens; chained, naked, beaten with rods, and lashed into obedience." Her exposé caused a public outcry and a reform bill was passed. That same year her book, *Prison and Prison Discipline*, appeared.

This success launched Dix's lifelong career as a prison reformer. She traveled state to state visiting various institutions, studying their needs and enlisting the help of philanthropists and politicians to renovate or build facilities and improve treatment. Dix also founded new hospitals or additions in five northeastern states and Canada and received authorization from state legislatures to set up state hospitals in 10 other states, from Maryland to Missouri.

In 1848, Dix visited the British Isles and found Scottish institutions in need of reform, so she presented a case to the advocate of Scotland. In Rome, she met with Pope Pius to share her concerns about Italy's inadequate facilities. He ordered construction of a new hospital and revised rules for care of the mentally ill. Before returning to the United States, Dix inspected hospitals and prisons in Austria, Belgium, France, Germany, Greece, Holland, Russia, Scandinavia and Turkey and recommended improvements.

In 1861, Dix was appointed superintendent of women nurses during the **Civil War (1861-1865)**. After the war, she resumed her reform efforts until her death at age 85 in Trenton, New Jersey.

Dorothea Dix.

Born in Litchfield, Connecticut, the seventh of 13 children of Presbyterian minister **Lyman Beecher (1175-1863)** and his wife **Roxana**, abolitionist and author **Harriet Beecher Stowe's** famous siblings include her older sister, education pioneer **Catherine Beecher** (see page 42) and abolitionist **Henry Ward Beecher** (1813-1887). In 1832, she accompanied her father to his new post as president of Lane Theological Seminary in Cincinnati and married **Calvin Stowe**, a professor and ardent opponent of slavery, in 1836. Her first book was *The Mayflower* (1843).

For 18 years, Stowe lived across the Ohio River from Kentucky, a slave-holding state. Moved by the despair of fugitive slaves and believing she had a religious message to deliver, she wrote a serialized tale in 40 installments for the Washington, DC-based anti-slavery paper, *The National Era*, entitled *Uncle Tom's Cabin, or, Life Among the Lowly* about how slavery was destroying black family life. Published as a

Harriet Beecher Stowe.

book on March 20, 1852, *Uncle Tom's Cabin* so aroused the national conscience against slavery that it served to hasten the onset of the **Civil War (1861-1865)**. Though not a great literary work, it stands as perhaps the single most influential book in American history.

The success of *Uncle Tom's Cabin* was unprecedented. In the five years following its publication, it sold 500,000 copies in the United States and was translated into more than 20 languages. In 1853, Stowe published *A Key to Uncle Tom's Cabin*, which contained a wealth of documentary evidence to support the militant anti-slavery stance of her previous book. That same year, she journeyed to Europe to lecture against slavery. In 1856, another anti-slavery book, *Dred: A Tale of the Dismal Swamp*, appeared.

Harriet Beecher Stowe lived out her life as a woman of letters, writing several more novels and a volume of religious poetry, occasionally giving public readings of her works. She died in Hartford, Connecticut, at the age of 85.

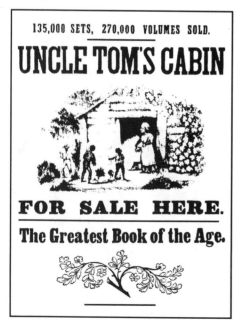

135,000 SETS, 270,000 VOLUMES SOLD.

UNCLE TOM'S CABIN

FOR SALE HERE.

The Greatest Book of the Age.

38. ADA LOVELACE
1815-1852

Born in London, England, mathematician and pioneer computer scientist **Ada Byron** was the daughter of poet **Lord George Byron (1788-1824)** and **Annabella Millbanke**, whom Bryon once referred to as the "Princess of Parallelograms" because of her interest in mathematics. Shortly after her birth, Lord Byron left his family and Ada never saw him again. At age 19 she married the **Earl of Lovelace**.

In 1833, Lovelace and family friend **Mary Fairfax Somerville** (see page 38) viewed a model of the **Difference Engine** in the studio of inventor and scientist **Charles Babbage (1792-1871)**. After studying finite differences—the mathematical basis of Babbage's invention—Lovelace initiated an 18-year correspondence with him, during which she progressed from being his student to being his collaborator. In 1842, she translated a paper by Italian mathematician **L.F. Menabrea** on the function and theory of Babbage's newest invention, the **Analytical Engine**, adding her own annotations and seven notes which greatly elaborated on the original. Lovelace's work was so superior to Menabrea's, Babbage encouraged her to publish it as a separate paper, which she did in *Taylor's Scientific Memoirs* (1843). She signed it "A.L.L.," as in her day, it would have been unseemly for a noblewoman to take credit for such a work. Her identity remained secret from the public for the next 30 years.

In her notes, Lovelace made a detailed comparison of Babbage's two inventions. Whereas the Difference Engine could merely tabulate, the Analytical Engine could both tabulate and develop. She also described how to feed information into the Engine on punched cards. As in modern **computer punch cards**, the patterns of the holes corresponded to mathematical sym-

Ada Lovelace.

bols. In another remarkable note, Lovelace predicted the future possibility of **computerized music**, stating that music itself is mathematical and thus adaptable to being composed by a machine.

Babbage's invention never progressed past the planning stage due to a lack of money and the fact that his design was too far advanced for the precision engineering of the time. However, by the mid-twentieth century, he would be recognized as the father of modern computers and Ada Lovelace as the first person to fully describe the process now known as **computer programming**. In the 1980s, in recognition of Lovelace's pioneering achievements, the US Department of Defense named its new systems implementation programming language **Ada**. Ada Lovelace died of cancer at the age of 36.

39-40. CHARLOTTE BRONTË 1816-1855 and EMILY BRONTË 1818-1848

Charlotte and Emily were born in Yorkshire at Thornton, England. Their Irish father, Patrick Brontë, who himself was the author of two volumes of verse, served as a rector at Haworth until his death in 1861. After their mother, Maria Branwell, died of cancer in 1821, her sister Elizabeth came to care for the family. The children were often left alone to amuse themselves and they spent their time reading, walking the moors and writing an enormous amount of juvenile literature. In the span of 15 months, Charlotte wrote 23 "novels," which, though of no consequence now, demonstrate the depth of her creative energy.

Together with their sister Anne (1820-1849) and brother Patrick, the sisters created a series of stories about two imaginary kingdoms called Angria, which belonged to Charlotte and Patrick, and Gondal, which was the property of Emily and Anne. One hundred handwritten chronicles about Angria, started in 1829, still survive today, although only a few of Emily's poems from the Gondal series exist. For one year Charlotte and Emily and their two elder sisters, Maria and Elizabeth, attended the Clergy Daughters' School at Cowen's Bridge. The horrors they experienced there—inadequate food and overly harsh discipline—were later described by Charlotte in *Jane Eyre*, in which she called the school Lowood.

In 1842, Charlotte and Emily, with the idea of eventually opening their own school, went to school in Brussels to improve their French but were quickly called home due to the death of their aunt. Charlotte later returned to Brussels and her experience there formed the basis for her novel *Villette* (1852), a story powered by the intense loneliness of its heroine. Upon her return to Haworth, she and Emily attempted to set up a tutoring business in

Charlotte Brontë.

their home but their advertisements failed to draw any pupils. This disappointment was compounded by their brother's complete collapse. A failed painter who had been dismissed from several positions, Patrick became an alcoholic and opium addict.

In 1846, Charlotte discovered Emily's poems, which prompted them, along with Anne, to jointly self-publish their verses, using pseudonyms based on the letters of their first names. The volume, *Poems by Currer, Ellis and Acton Bell*, sold two copies. Undeterred, each set about writing a novel. Charlotte's *Jane Eyre*, a portrait of a governess on a remote estate belonging to a moody, tormented man, appeared first. Later the same year, Anne's *Anne Grey* and Emily's *Wuthering Heights* were published. Patrick died in September 1848 from the effects of his prolonged alcoholism. Emily died in December of tuberculosis. Anne died the following May of the same disease. Her second novel, *The Tenant of Wildfell Hall* (1848), which described an alcoholic's decline, contained many autobiographical elements.

Charlotte went on to complete two more novels: *Shirley* (1849), a realistic drama concerning workers and their masters in the weaving industry a generation before, and *The Professor* (1857). In 1854, she married her father's curate, Arthur Nicolls. While pregnant the following year, she died of tuberculosis.

The work of the reclusive Brontë sisters, most notably *Jane Eyre* and *Wuthering Heights*, have become enduring literary classics because their timeless themes transcend the Victorian era in which they were written. Anne Brontë's work, though less known, should not be discounted, for by her presence and interaction she added greatly to the literary milieu in the Bronte household.

Jane Eyre, because it does not conform to the realm of conventional "women's fiction" of the time, is considered one of the most stirring depictions of feminism in English literature. *Wuthering Heights*, hauntingly grim and melancholy in tone, reveals the mystical side of Emily's personality. Both are stories of passionate love, which portray their female heroines as flaunting the traditional societal belief that women were merely the loved and not the lovers, a theme many of their Victorian readers surely found to be a bit shocking—but irresistible.

Emily Brontë's *Wuthering Heights* is considered a literary classic.

Born in Johnston, New York, as the daughter of Judge **Daniel Cady**, women's rights activist **Elizabeth Cady Stanton** observed firsthand the tragic effects of discriminatory laws against women and she became determined to fight for equality. By circulating petitions, she was instrumental in the passage of an 1848 New York law granting property rights to women. Through her work in the antislavery movement, she met **Henry Stanton**, a journalist and antislavery orator. They married in 1840 and had eight children.

In 1840, Stanton began working with **Lucretia Coffin Mott** (see page 41), and in 1848 they organized the first **Women's Rights Convention** at Seneca Falls, New York, which included many male sympathizers. Stanton, a gifted writer, drafted a *Declaration of Sentiments*—patterned after the **Declaration of Independence**—stating that men and women were created equal and demanding, for the first time publicly, that women be granted voting rights.

In 1851, Stanton began a 50-year collaboration on antislavery and feminist causes with **Susan B. Anthony** (see page 52), during which Stanton provided the ideas and written works and Anthony provided the oratorical and organizational talent. From 1858 to 1860, they published a weekly New York newspaper, *Revolution*, edited by Stanton, which was devoted to publicizing incidents of unequal treatment of women.

After the **Civil War (1861-1865)**, male abolitionists voiced fears that the demands of women suffragists would jeopardize the campaign to secure voting rights for male ex-slaves. In response, Stanton and Anthony created the **National Woman Suffrage Association** in 1869 to deal specifically with the issue of securing national voting rights for women and Stanton served as its

Elizabeth Cady Stanton.

president until 1892. Besides Stanton and Anthony, the association included many other leading activists such as **Jane Addams** (see page 67), **Clara Barton** (see page 55), **Carrie Chapman Catt** (see page 66), **Julia Ward Howe** (1819-1910) and **Harriet Beecher Stowe** (see page 44).

In 1888, Stanton and Anthony helped found the **International Council of Women** to coordinate suffragist efforts worldwide. In conjunction with Stanton, **Ida Harper** and **Matilda Gage**, she worked on the first three volumes of *The History of Woman Suffrage* (6 volumes, 1881-1922). She died in New York City at the age of 86.

42. LUCY STONE
1818-1893

Growing up in Brookfield, Massachusetts, women's rights activist **Lucy Stone** was deeply disturbed over the long hours of hard work imposed on her mother, who had even been required to milk eight cows the night before Lucy was born. In order to determine if Biblical scriptures approving the subjugation of women were correctly translated, she resolved to go to college to study Greek and Hebrew. After saving money for nine years, she entered Oberlin College in Ohio—then the only American institution admitting women—at age 25. Because she had to work in order to pay tuition, she would arise at 2:00 a.m. to study. Her outspoken views rankled some of the faculty, but she graduated first in her class in 1847.

In 1848, she was hired as a lecturer for the **Anti-Slavery Society**, agreeing to appear at meetings on Saturday evenings and Sundays. During the week, she frequently lectured on women's rights. In 1855, she married the noted abolitionist **Henry Blackwell (1824-1909)**, brother of **Elizabeth Blackwell** (see page 56), and they issued a joint protest against the unfairness of marriage laws. As a symbol of her right to individuality, Stone, with her husband's full support, retained her maiden name after their marriage. Other women who followed her example became known as **Stoners**.

In 1869, **Susan B. Anthony** (see page 52) and **Elizabeth Cady Stanton** (see page 46) formed the **National Woman Suffrage Association** to seek a constitutional amendment granting women the right to vote. Stone, disagreeing with their strategy, formed the **American Woman Suffrage Association** in conjunction with **Henry Ward Beecher (1813-1887)** to work toward the gradual, state-by-state, adoption of women's suffrage. Later that year, Wyoming became the first state to grant women the right to vote. In 1890, the Stone-Beecher organization merged with the Anthony-Stanton group to become the **National American Woman Suffrage Association**. The organization continued to work toward the goal of women's suffrage on both the state and federal levels until Congress ratified the **Nineteenth Amendment** to the US Constitution in 1920 which gave American women the right to vote.

In 1870, Stone founded the *Woman's Journal*, which became the main publication of the women's suffrage movement. With the assistance of her husband, and later her daughter, she edited it until her death in 1893 at the age of 76. At that time, she achieved yet another first—she was the first woman in New England to be cremated.

Lucy Stone.

43. MARY ANN EVANS (GEORGE ELIOT) 1819-1880

Born in Chivers Coton, Warwickshire, England, the daughter of an estate agent, the childhood of author and essayist **Mary Ann Evans** was dominated by strict religious training. She attended boarding school until age 17 when her mother's death made it necessary for her to return home to keep house for her father. Always an avid reader, she eventually rebelled against oppressive orthodoxy and became known for her unconventional ways.

Evans' first work was a translation of *Das Lebe Jesu*, a German theological work. In 1851, after traveling in Europe for two years, she wrote a book review for the *Westminster Review*. Later, as an assistant editor at the publication, she met and worked with many leading English literary figures, including **Herbert Spencer (1820-1903), John Stuart Mill (1806-1883)** and philosopher and critic **George Lewes** (1817-1878). She and Lewes immediately fell in love. Unable to marry because Lewes' wife was insane (English law forbade a divorce under such circumstances), Evans and Lewes spent the next 24 years together, a mutually satisfying relationship which Evans viewed as a marriage. For his part, Lewes was extremely protective of her in later life, even shielding her from unfavorable literary reviews.

Evans began writing stories for *Blackwood's Magazine* and several were collected and published in 1858 as *Scenes from a Clerical Life* under her newly acquired pen name **George Eliot**, a pseudonym she employed for many years. This work made an immediate impression on the literary world and was highly praised by author **Charles Dickens (1812-1870)**, among others. There followed, in rapid succession, the publication of Evans' most well-known works: *Adam Bede* (1859), *The Mill on the Floss* (1860) and *Silas Marner* (1861). Together, these highly realistic, autobiographical depictions of Victorian country life constitute Evans' most valuable contribution to English literature and our knowledge of English social history in the mid-nineteenth century.

Evans wrote numerous other essays, books and poems until Lewes death in 1878, when she became a recluse and ceased to write. These later works were also well-received among her contemporaries. Of particular note is her novel *Daniel Denonda* (1876), a strongly worded indictment of anti-Semitism. In May 1880, she married American banker **John Cross**, a long time friend, but she died in London on December 22 of that same year.

Mary Ann Evans.

44. QUEEN VICTORIA
1819-1901

A woman intensely devoted to her duties as a wife, mother and queen, **Queen Victoria** became a living symbol of the greatness of the British Empire at the height of its glory. Her 64-year reign—the longest in English history—came to be called the **Victorian Age**, an era characterized by ardent nationalism and a return to conservative morality. Born in Kensington Palace, London, the only child of **Edward, duke of Kent**, the youngest brother of **William IV (1765-1837)**, and **Mary Louisa Victoria** of Saxe-Coburg-Gotha, at the age of 18 she succeeded her uncle to the throne when he died without an heir.

In 1840, Victoria married her cousin **Prince Albert, duke of Saxe-Coburg-Gotha (1819-1861)**. Though it was an arranged marriage, it proved to be a highly romantic and rewarding one. After his death in 1861, she spent three years in total seclusion and did not appear to open Parliament until 1864. She then continued to wear black and actively mourn Albert for the rest of her life.

The first of Victoria and Albert's nine children—also named Victoria—was born in 1840 and later became the empress of Germany. Queen Victoria's first grandchild was born in 1859 and her first great-grandchild was born in 1879. By the time of her death in 1901, she had 37 living great-grandchildren. Her descendants eventually ruled in Sweden, Denmark, Norway, Spain, Greece and Russia, thus earning her the affectionate title of the **Grandmother of Europe**.

Under Albert's considerable influence, Victoria exercised her full rights as a constitutional monarch "to be consulted, the right to encourage and the right to warn" her prime ministers. She became a strong supporter of the Conservative party, subsequently enjoying congenial relationships with prime ministers **Sir John Peel (1788-**

Queen Victoria.

1850) and **Benjamin Disraeli (1804-1881)**, who served in 1868 and from 1874-1880. Victoria fully endorsed Disraeli's plan to protect British foreign interests and to strengthen and increase the British Empire. In 1876, he had her crowned **Empress of India**. Conversely, she was continually at odds with the Liberal **William Gladstone (1808-1898)**, who served as prime minister four times between 1868 and 1894, because he favored reforms such as legalizing trade unions and Irish Home Rule.

During the **Crimean War (1854-1856)**, Victoria instituted the **Victoria Cross** for bravery and actively supported the pioneering work of nurse **Florence Nightingale** (see page 53). By the time she celebrated her diamond jubilee in 1897, her popularity had reached its height, both at home and abroad. She died at Osborne at the age of 82 and was buried beside Albert near Windsor.

45. SUSAN BROWNELL ANTHONY
1820-1906

A liberal Quaker and radical reformer, women's rights activist—known in her time as a suffragist—**Susan B. Anthony** devoted 50 years of her life to secure the right of American women to vote. As she stated in an 1873 address: "It was we the people, not we the white male citizens, nor yet we, the male citizens, but we, the whole people, who formed the Union."

Born in Adams, Massachusetts, the second of eight children, Anthony began teaching school at age 15, a career she continued for 15 years. She was strongly opposed to the use of liquor and took part in the temperance movement between 1848 and 1853, founding the first temperance society in America in New York in 1852. One of her greatest achievements was her ability to rally vast numbers of people of both sexes around a single goal. From 1856 to 1861 she used this talent in her work for the **Anti-Slavery Society**. During the **Civil War (1861-1865)**, she established the **Women's Loyal League** to work for the emancipation of slaves.

In 1851, **Elizabeth Cady Stanton** (see page 46) recruited Anthony for the women's suffrage movement. Between 1854 and 1860, they concentrated their efforts on reforming New York State's discriminatory laws. Convinced that true reforms would not occur until women had the right to vote, they founded the **American Woman Suffrage Association** in 1869 to work toward the passage of a constitutional amendment. Between 1858 and 1860, they published a weekly newspaper, *Revolution*, whose motto was "The true republic—men, their rights and nothing more; women, their rights and nothing less." In 1872, asserting that the Fifteenth Amendment to the Constitution entitled her to do so, Anthony cast a ballot in the presidential election. Arrested and fined $100, she defiantly refused to pay.

After meeting with activists in Europe, in 1888 Anthony and Stanton helped form the **International Council of Women** with representatives from 48 countries. In conjunction with Stanton, **Ida Harper** and **Matilda Gage**, Anthony worked on the first three volumes of *The History of Woman Suffrage* (6 volumes, 1881-1922). She continued speaking at conventions until her death in Rochester, New York, at the age of 86.

In 1878, Senator **A.A. Sargent** introduced a women's suffrage amendment known as the **Susan B. Anthony Amendment**, which languished for 42 years before being ratified as the **Nineteenth Amendment** on August 26, 1920. On July 2, 1979, in honor of her achievements, the US government issued the Susan B. Anthony coin dollar, making her the first American woman to have her picture on a circulated coin.

Susan Brownell Anthony.

Considered to be the founder of modern nursing, British nurse, hospital reformer and public health innovator **Florence Nightingale** was born in Florence, Italy, and raised in the countryside of Derbyshire, England. Believing she had a calling from God, she decided to dedicate her life to nursing. After traveling through Europe in 1849 to study hospital systems, she trained at the Institute of Saint Vincent de Paul in Alexandria, Egypt, and the Institute for Protestant Deaconesses at Kaiserswerth, Germany. In 1853, she used her allowance to reorganize the **Institution for the Care of Sick Gentlewomen** in Harley Street, London, gaining valuable experience in hospital administration.

In 1853, Russia invaded Turkey and ignited the **Crimean War (1854-1856)**. Aware of Nightingale's success in Harley Street, Britain's Secretary of War, **Sidney Herbert**, asked her to undertake a nursing mission in the Crimea. She and 38 nurses went to Uskudar (now part of Istanbul), where they found 5000 British soldiers housed in filthy, dilapidated buildings that not only lacked medical equipment but even the barest living essentials. Under Nightingale's direction, the nurses cleaned and disinfected the vermin-filled barracks. Each night, by the light of a lantern she carried, "The Lady with the Lamp" ended her 20-hour workday by personally inspecting every ward. Within months, casualties from infection dropped from 42 percent to 2.2 percent.

After the war, Nightingale returned to England as a national heroine. In 1857, encouraged by **Queen Victoria** (see page 51), Nightingale began the first scientific examination of the sanitary conditions and health of the peacetime army. Her book, *Notes on Matters Affecting the Health, Efficiency and Hospital Administration of the British Army*, remains the standard work of

Florence Nightingale.

its kind. She gradually widened the scope of her work to include civilian hospitals and public health.

In 1860, with money raised through donations, Nightingale founded the **Nightingale School of Nursing** at St. Thomas Hospital, the first professional nursing program in the world. Prior to this time, nursing was considered a menial job undertaken by untrained personnel who were often of dubious character. By establishing strict standards, Nightingale raised nursing to the level of a medical profession. She outlined her methods in *Notes on Nursing* (1859), the first textbook for nurses.

In 1907, Nightingale became the first woman to receive the British **Order of Merit**. After her death, the **Crimean Monument** was erected in her honor in Waterloo Place in London in 1915.

47. **HARRIET TUBMAN**
c. 1820-1913

Born **Araminta Ross** in 1820 near Cambridge, Maryland, one of 11 children of **Benjamin and Harriet (Green) Ross, Harriet Tubman** took her mother's first name. At age 13, she was seriously wounded by a two-pound weight when she intervened between a fleeing slave and an overseer. During her convalescence, she began to question the workings of a society in which she had no power.

In 1844, she married **John Tubman**, a free black, but when she escaped north in 1849, he remained behind. In Philadelphia, she supported herself by working as a cook and domestic, and after saving enough money, she traveled south and led her sister **Mary Ann Bowley** and her two children to freedom. By 1857, she had freed her entire family.

Carrying a long rifle—to encourage fleeing slaves who had second thoughts as well as to defend against attack—Tubman made 19 trips, leading an estimated 300 people to freedom in Canada along an "underground" network of "safe houses" that became known as the **Underground Railroad**. She became so notorious that rewards for her capture totaled $40,000. She was financially supported in her work by many leading activists of the day. One ally, **William Sill** of the **General Vigilance Committee**, an abolitionist group, wrote of her: "... in point of courage, shrewdness and disinterested exertions to rescue her fellow man, she was without equal." To her own people, however, Tubman was known as **Moses**, for like the biblical character, she led them out of slavery to a better life.

Although historically Tubman is best remembered for her work on the Underground Railroad, she was also a nurse, a spy and an outspoken feminist reformer. During the **Civil War (1861-1865)**, she tended wounded soldiers and helped newly freed slaves learn self-sufficiency. On one

Harriet Tubman.

occasion, the US War Department directed her to organize a group of eight black men to scout the inland waterways of South Carolina in advance of the troops of Union General Richard Montgomery. Later she personally assisted General Montgomery during a raid.

After the war, Tubman moved to Auburn, New York, where she opened the **Harriet Tubman Home** for the aged and raised funds for schools for former slaves. She also enjoyed a long-time friendship with pioneer suffragist **Susan B. Anthony** (see page 52), with whom she was active in the **New England Anti-Slavery Society** and the **New England Suffrage Association**. In 1896, she was a speaker at the first annual convention of the **National Federation of Afro-American Women**. After a two-year residence in her retirement home, she died of pneumonia at the age of 93.

Known as the **Angel of the Battlefield** during the **Civil War (1861-1865)**, philanthropist **Clara Barton** was the founder of the **American Red Cross**. Born in Oxford, Massachusetts, she established several free schools in New Jersey, and during the Civil War she organized her own volunteers to distribute supplies to battlefields, even driving a four-mule wagon team herself. After the war, she set up a bureau of records in Washington, DC, to search for missing soldiers and identified and marked 12,000 graves at the National Cemetery at Andersonville, Georgia.

Between 1869 and 1873, Barton lived in Europe, where she founded military hospitals during the **Franco-Prussian War (1870- 1871)**, for which she was decorated with the Iron Cross by the German emperor. She also became acquainted with the work of the **International Red Cross**, begun by Swiss citizen **Henri Durant**, corecipient of the first **Nobel Peace Prize** in 1901.

In 1881, Barton organized the American Red Cross according to the 1863 **Treaty of Geneva**—that had set up guidelines for the international organization—and served as its president until 1904. Between 1884 and 1903, she represented the United States at the international convention four times and authored the "American amendment" to the Red Cross' constitution, which provided services in peacetime as well as in war. The **American Red Cross** was officially chartered in 1901 and again in 1905—a charter that is still in force.

Barton personally supervised Red Cross relief services during the yellow fever epidemic in Florida (1887), the infamous Johnstown (Pennsylvania) flood (1889), the Russian famine (1891), the Armenian massacre (1896), the **Spanish-American War (1898)** and the South African **Boer War (1899-1902)**.

Barton's books include *An Official History of the Red Cross* (1882), *The Red Cross in Peace and War* (1898) and her autobiography, *The Story of My Childhood* (1907). She died at Glen Echo, Maryland, at the age of 91.

Today, worldwide Red Cross services are organized into the following programs: 1) services to armed forces personnel and their families; 2) disaster relief and preparedness; 3) blood donation program (the largest in the world); 4) nursing and health assistance; 5) safety and first aid training; 6) youth leadership training; and 7) liaison work with the International Red Cross. Every year, more than one million volunteers are active in Red Cross work in America.

Clara Barton on the battlefield.

Elizabeth Blackwell, the first woman medical doctor in the United States, was born in Counterslip, Bristol, England, one of 12 children in a family of advocates of social reform. Her famous sisters-in-law included **Antoinette Brown Blackwell (1825-1921)**, the first ordained woman minister in America, and women's rights activist **Lucy Stone** (see page 49). In 1832, after a fire destroyed her father's refinery, the family emigrated to New York, where all the Blackwells became involved in the antislavery movement, offering their home as a haven for fugitive slaves.

When Blackwell was 17, her family moved to Cincinnati, Ohio, and her father died soon after. To support their mother and nine surviving children, the women

Elizabeth Blackwell.

operated a boarding school for four years. However, being a schoolteacher did not appeal to Blackwell. More as an expression of her resentment of social inequalities than from a passion for medicine, Blackwell decided to become a physician. As she stated in her autobiography (1895), "The idea of winning a doctor's degree gradually assumed the aspect of a great moral struggle."

Rebuffed by numerous schools including Harvard and Yale, Blackwell entered Geneva Medical College, graduating first in her class in 1849. Her first practical experience occurred in 1848 when she helped to combat a typhoid epidemic. She later wrote her thesis on this subject. After receiving her degree, she studied at St. Bartholomew's Hospital in London and on the continent, returning to New York in 1851. Ostracized in her attempts to set up a medical practice, she and her sister **Emily Blackwell**, also a physician, bought a house in a slum area with the aid of Quaker friends and opened the **New York Infirmary for Indigent Women and Children** (later **New York Infirmary**). From its inception, the Infirmary always had an entirely female staff, the first such institution ever founded. A medical college was added in 1868 and **Sophia Jex-Blake** (see page 61) was the first student to register.

Leaving the operation of the Infirmary to her sister Emily, she returned to England in 1869, where she became one of the founders of the **National Health Society of London**. In 1874, jointly with Jex-Blake, she founded the London School of Medicine for Women, where she was a professor of gynecology from 1875 to 1907. Her writings include *The Physical Education of Girls* (1852) and her autobiography, *Pioneer Work in Opening the Medical Profession to Women* (1895). She died at Hastings, England, at the age of 89.

50. MARY BAKER EDDY
1821-1910

As the founder of the **Church of Christ, Scientist (Christian Science), Mary Baker Eddy** developed a system of religious philosophy so unique, that even today it is seen as being outside the mainstream of traditional Christian belief. Born near Concord, New Hampshire, she was a sickly child who had to be tutored at home. Even after the birth of her only child in 1843, her continuing poor health kept her confined to home, where she ran a school.

Eddy's interest in religious healing first surfaced when she was 12. As she lay sick with a fever, her mother exhorted her to pray. "I prayed, and a soft glow...came over me," she reported later. "The fever was gone..." In 1862, still suffering chronic ill health, she consulted **Phineas Parkhurst Quimby**, a spiritual healer. Finding relief after he prayed with her, she adopted his philosophy that disease could be cured by spiritual concentration.

However, her discovery of Christian Science resulted from an accident that occurred in 1866. Eddy slipped on an icy street and severely injured herself. On the third day of her convalescence, she read this account in Matthew 9:2 and experienced an immediate recovery: "And behold they brought to Jesus a paralytic lying on a pallet. And Jesus, seeing their faith, said to the paralytic, 'Take courage, son; thy sins are forgiven thee.' "

After this, Eddy regarded the Bible as a "textbook" that could make her understand the nature of her healing. As she wrote in the main study text for her new religion, *Science and Health with a Key to the Scriptures* (1879), "I apprehended for the first time, in their spiritual meaning, Jesus' teaching...and the Principle and rule of spiritual Science and metaphysical healing—in a word, Christian Science." Eddy also wrote a dozen other religious works, including her autobiography, *Retrospection and Introspection*.

Eddy's thinking appealed to many people, especially women, who found little relief from medical science. After she founded the **Christian Science Association** in 1875, she became the first practitioner and teacher of her philosophy, supervising every phase of the growing Christian Science movement. In 1881, she opened the **Massachusetts Metaphysical College** to train other practitioners, or mental healers, charging $300 for a course of study. The **First Church of Christ, Scientist** was opened in Boston, Massachusetts, in 1892. In that same year she founded the **Christian Science Publishing Society**, and in 1908, the *Christian Science Monitor* was first published. When she died at her home near Boston at the age of 89, she left an estate worth $2.5 million.

Mary Baker Eddy.

51. LAKSHMI BAI, RANI OF JHANSI
c. 1830-1858

Lakshmi Bai (läk'shmē bī') became an Indian national heroine when she died for the cause of justice while leading her troops during the **Indian Mutiny**. Born in India as **Manukarnika** (a name for the sacred Ganges River), the daughter of a Brahmin official, she grew up with her brothers and father, who taught her martial arts and how to ride a horse.

Upon her marriage to Rajah **Gangadhar Rao** of Jhansi, she changed her name to **Lakshmi**, the goddess of fortune. When she and her husband were unable to have a son, they adopted his cousin. After Gangadhar died in 1853, the Governor-General, the **Marquess of Dalhousie**, announced that since there was no heir— adoption did not count—the colonial British government planned to annex Jhansi. This decision flew in the face of Hindu religious belief that an adopted son was equally capable of performing the ritual sacrifices necessary to spare his father the fires of Put (hell).

Indian historians later cited Dalhousie's annexation policy as one of the main causes of the Indian Mutiny, also known as the **Sepoy Rebellion**. (Sepoys were native troops serving in non-Indian armies.) Another causal factor was the fact that westernization threatened to overthrow the existing caste system and undermine the authority of the Brahmins (orthodox Hindus of the highest caste).

Lakshmi sent two petitions to appeal Dalhousie's decision. When he turned them down in February 1854, she hired a British counsel and appealed to London. That appeal was also refused, and she then retired from public view for three years.

By 1857, the Mutiny was well underway and on July 7, the sepoys massacred British civilians at **Star Fort**. Although Lakshmi was forced under threat of death to give the rebels money and elephants, the

Lakshmi Bai.

British believed her to be guilty of being involved in the massacre. Thus in March 1858, the British laid siege to the city of Jhansi. Lakshmi, who remained constantly visible to both her troops and the enemy in the thick of the battle, was able to escape shortly before the city fell. Lakshmi rode to the city of Kalpi, where she was given a heroine's welcome. Putting on armor and a sword with a jeweled scabbard, she led her troops on a successful mission to recapture the neighboring fortress of Gwalior. However, when British reinforcements attacked, she was killed during hand-to-hand combat while defending the city.

Statues in her honor have been erected at Jhansi and **Gwalior**, and her memory has been preserved in numerous folk ballads such as this one: "The song of joy, the song of freedom rises/In every corner of the land this song is heard/Here fought Lakshmi Bai..." During the nationalist movement in the twentieth century that culminated in India's independence in 1947, Lakshmi Bai became an inspirational symbol of Indian bravery and patriotism.

Clad in a black bonnet and dress with a lace collar, she became a familiar sight to striking workers across America during the late nineteenth and early twentieth centuries. Called **Mother Jones** by those she organized to strike for better wages and working conditions, **Mary Harris** was born in Cork, Ireland, and emigrated to Canada when she was five. In 1861, she married ironworker and unionist **George Jones**, who along with their four children died in an 1867 epidemic. After the **Great Chicago Fire of 1871** destroyed all her possessions, she became involved in labor organizing.

In 1877, Jones joined the striking workers of the **Baltimore & Ohio Railroad** and watched as they set fire to 100 freight cars, causing $5 million in damages. In the early 1880s, she became a fiery orator for **United Mine Workers**, crisscrossing the country to tell men to "Join the Union!" In 1898 she was a founding member of the **Social Democratic Party**.

Mary Harris Jones.

Mine owners often hired "scabs" to replace striking workers. In Arnot, Pennsylvania, Jones organized a brigade of miners' wives to wait outside the mine. When mule-carts brought them out, the women began screaming and banging dishpans, and the animals bolted in fear. Another time, when her brigade was jailed, Jones instructed them to sing continuously in their cells. After five days, they were released.

By 1905, three-quarters of all miners belonged to the union. In 1907, Jones was the only woman invited to attend the founding meeting of the **International Workers of the World (IWW)**, or **Wobblies**. After a Virginia strike in 1911, she was sentenced to 20 years' imprisonment for conspiracy, but was reprieved by the governor. When she was jailed following a march in Denver, Colorado, a workers revolt on her be-

half resulted in the 1914 **Ludlow Massacre** where National Guard troops killed 13 women and children. By publicizing this atrocity nationwide, she was able to galvanize public opinion in the miners' favor.

Jones was also a strong advocate of legislation to prohibit child labor, and in 1915 she headed a march of child laborers from their Pennsylvania textile plant to the home of President Theodore Roosevelt (1858-1919) in New York so "he could hear the wail of children who never had a chance to go to school." A state law was subsequently passed that barred children under 14 from performing factory work.

Between 1915 and 1919, Harris supported the New York garment workers' and streetcar workers' strikes before joining the 1919 steelworkers' strike. In 1921, at the age of 91, she attended a meeting of the **Pan-American Federation of Labor** in Mexico, where she got a resolution passed to free all political prisoners. When she died at the age of 100, she was buried near the graves of strike victims in the coalfields of southern Illinois.

53. LOUISA MAY ALCOTT
1832-1888

Her father was philosopher and visionary educator **Amos Bronson Alcott (1799-1888)**, whose revolutionary teaching methods inspired ridicule and brought financial ruin to his family. Nonetheless, **Louisa May Alcott**, who was born in Germantown (later part of Philadelphia), Pennsylvania, and raised in Boston, enjoyed a happy childhood growing up with her four sisters. She was tutored by philosopher **Ralph Waldo Emerson (1803-1882)** (a close family friend) and writer **Henry David Thoreau (1817-1862)**. Jurist **Oliver Wendell Holmes (1841-1935)** and writer **Nathaniel Hawthorne (1804-1864)** often visited her home. Her backyard playhouse included diaries and dictionaries, which she learned how to use before she was five years old. In this atmosphere, she developed strong opinions on politics and social reform.

To help with family finances, Alcott worked at various jobs, including making doll dresses, teaching and domestic service. At that time, wild, sensational stories, known as **pot-boilers**, could earn five or 10 dollars, so she tried her hand at writing stories with titles like *Whispers in the Dark*, which were later published in her collected works. Her first book, *Flower Fables* (1854), was a collection of tales originally written for Emerson's daughter Ellen.

During the **Civil War (1861-1865)**, Alcott volunteered as a nurse in Washington, DC, supporting herself as a seamstress and governess. The letters she wrote to her family during this period were published as *Hospital Sketches*, first as a serial in *Commonwealth* magazine and then as a book in 1863, and established her reputation as a writer. In 1868, she became editor of a magazine for young girls called *Merry's Museum*.

Alcott's most famous work, *Little Women* (1868), an autobiographical novel about her childhood which depicts warm and funny family relationships, is one of the most enduringly popular children's book ever written and sold 87,000 copies within three years. This book and its sequel, *Little Men*, which introduced readers to her nephews, are considered children's classics. Her other works include *Moods* (1864), *An Old Fashioned Girl* (1870), *Work* (1873), *Spinning Wheel Stories* (1884) and *Jo's Boys* (1886), and numerous short stories and sketches.

Alcott was also active in the causes of abolition and women's suffrage. She died in Boston in 1888 at the age of 55.

Louisa May Alcott.

A committed and forceful advocate of a woman's right to practice medicine in the British Isles, **Sophia Jex-Blake** became the first woman medical doctor in Scotland. She was born in Hastings, England, the youngest daughter of a proctor of Doctors' Commons, and in 1858, she entered Queen's College in London, where she was a tutor in mathematics while pursuing her degree. When she was 25, she sailed to Boston to observe American teaching methods. She recorded her impressions in *A Visit To Some American Schools and Colleges* (1867).

Jex-Blake became interested in medicine as a "cause worth fighting for and a field of service that should be open to all women" and applied to Harvard and other medical schools. When she was turned away, she became the first student to enroll at the Women's Medical College of the New York Infirmary founded by **Elizabeth Blackwell** (see page 56). However, after only a year, her studies were postponed due to her father's death. In 1869, after the University of London refused to admit her, she and four other women, following a strenuous campaign, were allowed to enroll at the University of Edinburgh. However, they were refused permission to study at the Royal Infirmary, a necessary step to completing a degree. When the women tried to enter the Infirmary, male students blocked their way, and a riot ensued. This incident—plus the fact that although a woman had placed first in the Hope Scholarship exam, a man was awarded the prize—aroused public sentiment in the women's favor. Officials then declared that women could only receive "certificates of proficiency" not diplomas. The women filed suit and three years later in 1876 the **Russel Gurney Enabling Act** allowed women to be tested for graduation.

Meanwhile, in 1874 Jex-Blake and Elizabeth Blackwell had founded the **London School of Medicine for Women**. In 1877, Jex-Blake graduated from the University of Berne and was allowed to practice medicine in England. The following year she returned to Edinburgh, where she opened a dispensary, which in 1886 became the **Edinburgh Hospital for Women and Children**, making her the first woman doctor in Scotland. In 1888, she organized the **Edinburgh School of Medicine for Women**. In 1894, largely through her influence, the University of Edinburgh accorded women students full rights and she then closed her school because it was no longer needed. She chronicled her and other women's experiences in *Medical Women* (1886). She died at Rotherfield, Sussex, England, at the age of 71.

55. ANNIE BESANT
1847-1933

Annie Besant.

Fellow **Fabian Society** member and dramatist **George Bernard Shaw (1856-1950)** once described social activist **Annie Besant** (bĕz′ənt) as "...a sort of expeditionary force [whose] displays of personal courage and resolution [compelled people] to listen by sheer force of style and character." These qualities of character would lead Besant into a reform career that spanned 50 years and two continents.

Born in London, Besant became involved in socialist causes that included publishing a pamphlet advocating birth control, for which she was imprisoned on a charge of "obscenity." In 1885, she joined the Fabian Society, a group founded in 1884 to work for social change through legislative means, and became known as a gifted orator. As a journalist, she became aware of the plight of blue collar workers, many of whom were jobless due to a decade-long economic depression. On November 17, 1887—**Bloody Sunday**—she took part in a workers' march, which was dispersed by police on horseback wielding truncheons, an experience which intensified her commitment to fight poverty and oppression.

"Match girls" at the **Bryant & May** factory in the East End of London made matches while standing at benches for up to 10 hours a day, under the threat of heavy fines for mistakes and at risk for **phossy jaw**—a lethal decay of the gums caused by the phosphorus in matches. In June 1888, Besant organized the walkout of 1400 match girls and whipped up public support in the press by comparing the workers' paltry earnings with the company's hefty profits. After a month-long strike, the women won a generous settlement and formed the 700-woman **Union of Women Matchmakers**. Their success helped stimulate the growth of other women's unions and also put pressure on male trade unionists to accept women as equals. In the next eight years, the number of women trade unionists grew from 40,000 to 118,000. In 1889, Besant joined the **Theosophical Society** headed by Russian spiritualist **Helen Blavatsky** (blə-văt′skē) **(1831-1891)**, who espoused a mystical philosophy based on Indian religious thought, and she served as its president from 1907 until her death. When she moved to India, she learned the Sanskrit language and established the **Central Hindu College** in Benares in 1898. After becoming active in the Indian independence movement, in 1916, she founded the **Home Rule India League** (1916) and edited *New India*, a daily paper in Madras. She also served as the fifth president of the **Indian National Congress** from 1917 to 1923, a unique position for an Englishwoman. Her books include *Autobiography* (1893) and *India, Bond or Free?* (1926). Besant died in Madras, India, at the age of 86.

Born in New York City, the daughter of a wealthy family, poetess **Emma Lazarus** (lăz′ər-əs) was surrounded by literature and fine art as a child. Her first work, *Admetus and Other Poems*, was inscribed to her mentor **Ralph Waldo Emerson (1803-1882)** and was published in 1866 when she was only 17 years old. Her next book was a romance entitled *Alide* (1874). She wrote numerous magazine articles and in 1881 *Poems and Ballads of Heinrich Heine* appeared. Angered by the persecution of Russian Jews in the early 1880s, Lazarus became an ardent Zionist and in 1882 published *Song of a Semite*, which was a militant call to arms. This collection of works included her translations of medieval Jewish poems and a religious drama, *The Dance of Death*, based on an accusation that Jews had caused Europe's **Black Death** in the **Middle Ages** by poisoning well water.

Lazarus is most well remembered for her sonnet, *The New Colossus* (1883), which she donated for an auction to raise money for the **Statue of Liberty** fund. The poem was then inscribed on a tablet near the base of the statue. Unveiled on October 28, 1886, the statue, located on **Liberty Island** (formerly **Bedloe's Island**) at the entrance to New York harbor, is that of a woman in flowing robes wearing a spiked crown who holds a lit torch aloft with her right arm and clutches a book in her left engraved with the words "July 4, 1776."

The Statue of Liberty is made of copper and iron, and together the statue and its pedestal rise over 305 feet from the ground, making it one of the tallest such monuments in the world. A gift from the government of France given as a gesture of international friendship to the United States, the Statue of Liberty has become the most well-known symbol of freedom in the world. Between 1892 and 1954, over 12 million immigrants were filled with hope at the sight of the statue, which greeted them on their way to **Ellis Island**.

Lazarus died in New York City in 1887 at the age of 38, but her poem about the Statue of Liberty, her legacy, lives on, expressing her ardent belief that the United States was a safe haven for the oppressed. The last, and most famous, lines of her verse are:

Give me your tired, your poor,
Your huddled masses yearning to breathe free,
The wretched refuse of your teeming shore.
Send these, the homeless, tempest-tost to me,
I lift my lamp beside the golden door!

Emma Lazarus.

57-58. EMMELINE PANKHURST 1858-1928 and CHRISTABEL PANKHURST 1880-1958

Emmeline Pankhurst, the matriarch of Britain's most militant family of women's rights activists, was born in Manchester and attended her first suffrage meeting with her mother at the age of 14. In 1879 she married **Richard Pankhurst**, a barrister who drafted Britain's first women's suffrage bill and later the **Married Women's Property Act of 1882** for political economist **John Stuart Mill (1806-1873)**. After Richard died in 1898 leaving her with four children, she became the Registrar in Rushholme, a working-class district of Manchester. Observing the legal and social oppression of women, she decided that only equal political rights could emancipate women and reform society as a whole.

In 1903, Emmeline became disillusioned with the **Independent Labor Party's (ILP)** lack of progress towards securing women's suffrage and formed her own organization, the **Women's Social and Political Union (WSPU)**, with her three daughters **Christabel, Sylvia (1882-1960)** and **Adela (1885-1961)** under the slogan "Votes for Women."

Christabel attended school in Manchester and Switzerland. In 1901, while studying law at Victoria University, she became a member of the **North of England Society for Women's Suffrage** and the **Manchester Women's Trade Union Council**. In 1905, after two years of active campaigning, she and mill worker **Anne Kenney** were arrested for protesting at a Liberal Party meeting in 1905. Offered a small fine or jail, the women chose jail, an action which catapulted the WSPU into national prominence.

Meanwhile, Emmeline moved to London to live with Sylvia, an artist. Sylvia later founded WSPU branches in the East End of London between 1912 and 1913, from which she eventually formed a separate organization, the **East London Feder-**ation. In 1935, she published *The Life of Emmeline Pankhurst*. Adela, though initially involved with the WSPU, emigrated to Australia, where she helped organize the **Victoria Socialist Party** and was active in the **Australia First Movement**.

Christabel joined her mother in London in 1907 and for the next six years was the WSPU's chief organizer and orator. The WSPU's mass marches to the Houses of Parliament and disruption of official meetings brought an immediate response from police, and the ensuing newspaper coverage quickly spread their message across Britain. By 1908, frustrated by Prime Minister **Herbert Asquith**'s continued resistance and delaying tactics in Parliament, Emmeline and Christabel adopted more radical protest measures. They smashed windows in London's shopping district, burned letters in mailboxes, wrote "Votes for Women" in acid on golf course greens, chained themselves to gates outside the homes of government officials, defaced paintings and even burned an unoccupied building. However, their tactics were always aimed at property only and never endangered human lives.

Emmeline was arrested for the first time in 1908. Like other WSPU members, she chose jail over a fine and then went on a hunger strike. By the time of her conviction in 1913 for incitement to violence (for which she received a three-year sentence), the government had passed the **Prisoners Temporary Discharge for Ill-Health Act**. Popularly known as the **Cat & Mouse Act**, it allowed hunger-striking prisoners to be temporarily released until they regained their strength. Rearrested 12 more times, Emmeline was reduced to such a state of weakness that after only a day or two on a hunger strike the government was forced to release her, as they couldn't risk having her die in custody.

In 1912, threatened with a conspiracy charge, Christabel fled to Paris, where she continued to direct WSPU strategy and publish *The Suffragette*. Her series of articles for this newspaper on venereal disease, which by the standards of the time were quite outspoken, were later published as a book, *The Great Scourge*. During **World War I**, this book was reprinted as a guide for soldiers. Christabel eventually settled in California in 1940. Her last book, *Unshackled: The Story of How We Won the Vote*, was published in 1959.

The WSPU continued its militant campaign for women's suffrage until the outbreak of World War I in 1914, when its members redirected their energies toward the war effort.

That same year, Emmeline's autobiography, *My Own Story*, was published. She died in London in 1928, just one month before passage of the **Representation of the People Act** that granted full voting rights to all English women. Subsequently, in 1929 trade union leader **Margaret Bondfield (1873-1953)** became the first woman cabinet member in British history. Today, a statue of Emmeline stands in the Victoria Tower Gardens near the Houses of Parliament in London.

Emmeline and Christabel Pankhurst.

Born **Carrie Lane** in Ripon, Wisconsin, women's rights activist **Carrie Chapman Catt** graduated from Iowa State College and then worked as a teacher and principal in the schools of Madison City, Iowa, and as a journalist in San Francisco. After her husband **Leo Chapman** died, she returned to Iowa and married **George Catt**, an engineer, in 1890. In that same year, she began working on a suffrage campaign with **Susan B. Anthony** (see page 52) in South Dakota.

Known as an excellent administrator, Catt first served as chairperson of the **Or-ganization Committee of the National American Woman Suffrage Association (NAWSA)** from 1895 to 1899, when she succeeded Anthony as president, serving from 1900 to 1904. She was re-elected president in 1915, holding this post until her death 32 years later. In 1904, she helped organize the **International Woman Suffrage Alliance**, which held its first meeting in Berlin that year, and she served as its president from 1904 to 1923.

Between 1909 and 1915, Catt structured NAWSA along political district lines, so that while working for the vote women could receive training in political action techniques. Due in great part to Catt's ability to mobilize association members into an effective lobbying force, suffrage was granted in the states of Colorado (1893), Utah and Idaho (1896), Washington (1910), California (1911), Kansas, Oregon and Arizona (1912), Nevada and Montana (1914) and New York (1917). In 1920, national women's suffrage was granted when the **Nineteenth Amendment** to the US Constitution was ratified, which provided that "The right of citizens of the United States to vote shall not be denied or abridged by the United States or any state on account of sex." Later that year, Catt reorganized NAWSA, a two-million-member organization, as the **National League of Women Voters**.

In 1925, Catt brought together 11 national women's organizations to form the **National Committee on the Cause and Cure of War**, serving as president from 1925 to 1932. The purpose of this organization was to educate the American public about the United States' participation in world peace organizations. After **World War II**, her interest in world peace extended to the **United Nations**, where she used her influence to have qualified women named to various commissions.

Carrie Chapman Catt.

An exceptional writer, tireless social activist, committed worker for peace, champion of civil rights, social work pioneer and feminist, **Jane Addams** was one of the most influential women in American history. Born the eighth of nine children to a prosperous banker and miller in Cedarville, Illinois, she was deeply influenced by her family's abolitionist convictions and Quaker faith. In 1882, she graduated in the first class at the Rockford Seminary.

In 1889, Addams and **Ellen Starr (1860-1940)** opened **Hull-House**, the first settlement house in the United States. Located on Halstead Street in the heart of a factory district in Chicago, Illinois, Hull-House was staffed by Addams' college-educated contemporaries who provided a wide range of social services, including food, clothing and medical care, and leisure time activities. Hull-House quickly became a gathering place for people of all ages from the diverse surrounding community of mostly non-English-speaking immigrants. In the wake of the **Industrial Revolution**, Addams became a recognized leader in organized efforts to solve the social welfare needs of America's teeming cities. Many of her ideas were later incorporated into the **New Deal** policies of **President Franklin Roosevelt (1881-1945)**.

In 1912, Addams played a prominent role in founding the **National Progressive Party** and also organized the **Women's Peace Party**, serving as its chairperson in 1915. That same year she was elected president of the **International Congress of Women** at its meeting in The Hague and the president of the **Women's International League for Peace and Freedom**, serving as a delegate to congresses in Europe and the United States between 1919 and 1929. In 1920, she became one of the founders of the **American Civil Liberties Union (ACLU)**.

Her opposition to entering **World War I** caused her expulsion from the **Daughters of the American Revolution (DAR)**, who called her the "most dangerous woman in America today." However, Addams' strong peace stance was vindicated when President **Woodrow Wilson (1856-1924)** based his recommendations for postwar peace on her proposals. For her efforts, she shared the **1931 Nobel Peace Prize** with educator **Nicholas Murray Butler (1862-1947)**.

Her books include: *Democracy and Social Ethics* (1902), *Newer Ideals of Peace* (1907), *The Spirit of Youth and the City Streets* (1909), *Twenty Years at Hull-House* (1910), *A New Conscience and an Ancient Evil* (1911), *The Long Road of Woman's Memory* (1916), *Peace and Bread in Time of War* (1922), *The Second Twenty Years at Hull-House* (1930) and *The Excellent Becomes the Permanent* (1932).

Jane Adams.

Mary Kingsley.

Explorer **Mary Kingsley** was born in Highgate, London, the daughter of a wealthy doctor who traveled frequently to pursue studies in anthropology and natural history. Her only formal education was in German, which her father saw as useful for conducting research on his behalf. In 1892, after she had served as her mother's nurse-maid for 15 years, her parents died and her brother moved away. Left on her own for the first time in her life, Kingsley, then 29, took a holiday to the Canary Islands where traders' tales about Africa inspired her to continue her father's work.

In August 1893, Kingsley sailed from Liverpool aboard the *Lagos,* a small cargo ship, on the first of several trips to Africa. She had made an arrangement with the **British Museum** to collect specimens of river fish, and she brought back 65 species, many previously unknown, three of which the Museum named in her honor.

Kingsley based her expedition on trade, which not only gave her access to remote African tribes but made her financially independent. She deplored the European influence in Africa, particularly that of missionaries, who viewed natives as savages that needed to be "educated" rather than as people with a unique culture of their own that was worthy of respect. In her perspective, traders were more honorable, providing business opportunities for Africans without trying to recast their complex cultures in a European mold.

Exploring the Calabar and Ogowe rivers in the former Belgian Congo, she mixed freely with the **Fang**, a cannibal tribe, earning their respect by trading tobacco, pocket knives and colorful handkerchiefs in a forthright manner. As she described it in *Travels in Africa* (1897): "A certain sort of friendship arose... We each recognized that we belonged to that same section of the human race with whom it is better to

drink than to fight." An intrepid adventurer, she survived a fall into a spiked game pit, waded across leech-filled rivers and became the second climber to reach the top of Cameron Mountain, the highest point in West Africa. Upon her December 1895 return to England, Kingsley was hailed as a celebrity. Her second book, *West African Studies* (1889), was a powerfully written political tract that indicted the British government's policies in Africa and advocated cooperation between European and African cultures based on mutual respect. A detailed account of her journey can be found in D. Wilcox, *Ten Who Dared* (1977).

During the **Boer War** in 1899, Kingsley went to nurse Boer prisoners in Simonstown, Africa, where she contracted typhoid fever and died at the age of 37. At her request, she was buried at sea.

Physicist **Marja Sklodowska** was born in Warsaw, Poland, and received her early training from her father, who was a high school physics teacher. In 1891, she changed her first name to **Marie** and enrolled in the Sorbonne in Paris, where she ranked first in her class when she received her degree in physics. In 1895, she married physicist **Pierre Curie** (kyŏŏ-rē′) **(1859-1906)**. The Curies' study of **radioactive elements** contributed to an understanding of atoms and helped lay a foundation for modern **nuclear physics**.

Following the discovery of **X-rays** by **Wilhelm Roentgen (1845-1923)** in 1895 and **Henri Becquerel's (1852-1908)** discovery that uranium gave off similar invisible radiation in 1896, Marie began to measure the **uranium radiation** in pitchblende, coining the term **radioactive** to describe the elements in the ore that emitted radiation as their nuclei broke down. Her husband, physicist Pierre, who had been conducting studies on magnetism, joined Marie in her work. The elements they identified were **radium** and **polonium**, the latter named after Marie's native country of Poland. Over four years beginning in 1898, the Curies used a ton of pitchblende to study radium. In 1903, they shared the **Nobel Prize in physics** with Henri Becquerel, making Marie the first female Nobel Laureate.

After Pierre was run over and killed by a horse-drawn cart in 1906, Marie succeeded him as a professor of physics at the University of Paris, and in 1911 she was awarded an unprecedented second Nobel Prize, this time in chemistry, for her work on **radium compounds**, making her the first person to receive two Nobel Prizes. In 1914, she became head of the Paris Institute of Radium and co-founded the **Curie Institute**. Her published works include *Recherches sur les Substances Radioactives* (1904) and *Traite de Radioactivite* (1910). Marie Curie's final illness was diagnosed as pernicous anemia caused by overexposure to radiation. She died in Savoy in France at the age of 66.

The Curies' scientific legacy lived on in their daughter **Irene Curie-Joliot (1896-1956)** who, with her husband **Frederic Joliot (1900-1958)**, received the **1935 Nobel Prize** in chemistry for the artificial production of radioactive elements.

Marie Curie.

63. SARAH BREEDLOVE WALKER
1867-1919

During the **Reconstruction Era (1865-1898)** after the **Civil War (1861-1865)**, though no longer slaves, the lives of African-American sharecroppers changed little. Entrepreneur and philanthropist **Sarah Breedlove** was born in a window-less shack on a Louisiana plantation. After her parents died, she lived with her older sister, marrying at the age of 14 to escape her brother-in-law's abuse. In 1885, she had a daughter, **Lelia**, but became a widow two years later when her husband was killed by a lynch mob.

Using the traditional "wrap and twist" method to straighten her hair, Walker began to develop bald spots. By experimenting with patent medicines, she developed a formula which not only stopped her hair loss but fostered new growth. Starting with $1.50 worth of ingredients, she and other relatives filled jars with her hair preparation in the attic of her house. She then met and married **C.J. Walker**, a newspaper man who taught her advertising and mail order techniques.

Like most inventors, Walker's preparations were not totally original but improvements on existing products. However, she did invent the **hot comb** and **Wonderful Hair Grower**. She also was the first woman to organize supplies for black hair preparation, develop a steel comb with teeth spaced to comb hair easily, use mail order and organize door-to-door agents, and develop her own chain of beauty schools. By 1914, she became the first self-made woman millionaire in the United States. In 1908, Walker founded **Lelia College** in Pittsburgh to train cosmetologists, and in 1913 she opened a second school in New York City. By 1910, Walker had 5000 sales agents, each averaging $1000 a day in commissions. By 1919, she had 25,000 agents. Besides selling products, agents taught other women how to set up beauty

Sarah Breedlove Walker.

shops in their homes. Walker strongly promoted the idea of economic self-help. Walker believed that if a woman could run a business, she could manage her life.

Walker, who had never attended school, sent Lelia to Knoxville College. After building Villa Lewaro, her 34-room mansion on the Hudson River, she hired tutors for herself. An ardent believer in education, she donated money to several black institutions. She also became a social activist and supported causes that sought to combat racism.

Though a highly successful business-woman, Walker still had to deal with the male chauvinism of black males. Denied an opportunity to speak at the 1912 **National Negro Business League** convention, she pushed her way to the podium and with great fervor told the story of her rise from a cotton field in the South to building her own factory. At the 1913 convention, she served as a presenter on the program.

The daughter of **Sir Hugh Bell**, anthropologist and diplomat **Gertrude Margaret Lowthian Bell** spent her childhood in the countryside of Yorkshire, England, and graduated from Lady Margaret Hall College at Oxford University in 1887. Her archaeological career began with a visit to her uncle, **Sir Frank Lascelles**, then British Minister at Tehran in what is now Iran. Between 1899 and 1914, she made expeditions to the Arabian Peninsula and the Middle East. After these explorations were recorded in a number of works such as *Safar-Nama, Amurath to Amurath, Syria, the Desert and the Sown*, she became an acknowledged authority on the Middle East. She also was known for her translation of Arabic works. Throughout her life, she actively corresponded with a number of people, and in 1927 her letters were published in a two-volume collection entitled *The Letters of Gertrude Bell*.

In 1914, when the British assumed control over Iraq at the start of **World War I**, Bell went to work for the British intelligence service collecting information about Arab tribes. In 1917, she became an assistant to **Sir Percy Cox** in Baghdad, and in this capacity she became extremely influential in shaping the terms of postwar Iraq's independence from British administration.

In March 1921, **Winston Churchill (1874-1965)**, then Secretary of State for the colonies, organized the **Conference of Cairo** to set up an Arab government in Iraq. At the conference, which was attended by the principal British political and military officials of the Middle East, Bell played a key role in securing the ascension to the throne of King **Faisel I**. On her return to Baghdad, she was instrumental in bringing about the expulsion of Faisel's chief rival. For the next two years, she continued to assist Cox in helping to stabilize the newly installed government. King Faisel went on to guide Iraq to independence and membership in the League of Nations in 1932.

In 1923, her diplomatic work completed, Gertrude Bell was awarded the post of **Honorary Director of Antiquities** and became the moving force behind the establishment of an archaeological museum in Baghdad. She died there in 1926 at the age of 58.

Oxford University.

65. ALICE HAMILTON
1869-1970

A pioneer in industrial toxicology, **Alice Hamilton** chose research medicine because she wanted a career that would make her both useful and independent. After receiving her M.D. from the University of Michigan in 1893, she studied bacteriology and pathology at the University of Leipzig and the University of Munich (Germany), and at Johns Hopkins Medical School (Maryland).

In 1897, she became a professor of pathology at Northwestern University and for the next 10 years she lived at **Hull-House** founded by **Jane Addams** (see page 67). Observing conditions in the poverty-stricken factory district, she was outraged that unskilled laborers—most new immigrants—were forced by economic necessity to work in conditions that caused disease and death.

After being appointed to the **Illinois Commission on Occupational Diseases**, in 1910 Hamilton became the first American to combine modern laboratory procedures and field research to conduct a survey of industrial poisons. She identified 77 lead-using industries and 578 victims, which led to a ground-breaking state law that required safety measures and physical exams. As a special investigator for the **US Bureau of Labor**, Hamilton crusaded for public health and worker safety. By 1916, she was the leading American authority on lead poisoning and one of only a handful of industrial disease specialists.

In 1919, Harvard University invited Hamilton to become the first woman professor at their medical school (later the School of Public Health) because she was the only person qualified to teach a course in industrial medicine. After **World War I**, her role as a pioneer investigator changed to that of a consultant. A vocal activist and active solicitor of research funds, she was frequently called to testify on such issues as the reform of child labor laws and health insurance. Her book, *Industrial Poisons in the United States* (1925), the first text on the subject, made her one of two worldwide authorities in the field. Between 1924 and 1930, she served on the Health Committee of the **League of Nations** (later the **United Nations**).

In 1935, Department of Labor chief Frances Perkins (see page 78) hired Hamilton as a consultant in the newly formed **Division of Labor Standards**. It was in this capacity in 1937 that she conducted her last field survey—of the viscose rayon industry—which led to the passage of Pennsylvania's first compensation law for an occupational disease.

Hamilton's autobiography, *Exploring the Dangerous Trades*, appeared in 1943. In 1949, a revised version of her 1934 textbook *Industrial Toxicology* was published. Active into her eighties, she died at home of a stroke at the age of 101.

Alice Hamilton.

66. ROSA LUXEMBURG
1870-1919

Rosa Luxemburg.

One of the most important women in the history of international **socialism**, revolutionary **Rosa Luxemburg** was born in Zamosc in Russian Poland. As a teenager, she became interested in politics, and upon graduating from the Warsaw Gymnasium she joined the revolutionary Socialist party **Proletariat**. After fleeing to Switzerland in 1889 to avoid arrest, she earned her Ph.D. in economics from the University of Zurich with a thesis entitled *The Industrial Development of Poland.*

In 1893, with **Leo Jogiches**, Luxemburg founded the **Social Democratic Party of Poland and Lithuania**. She insisted that workers, rather than seeking Polish independence, should pursue the higher goal of overthrowing the tsar. In 1896, she became a member of the **German Social Democratic party (SPD)**, the largest and most influential in Europe, and in 1899, she joined the staff of *Vorwarts*, the daily Socialist paper. After being imprisoned in 1904, she returned to Poland to organize workers' strikes in Warsaw. Back in Berlin, she began a new career as an instructor of economics at a school for SPD officials (1907-1914) and published her extremely influential pamphlet *The Mass Strike*. She also wrote an economics textbook, and in 1914 she published her most famous work, *The Accumulation of Capital.*

Consistently opposed to nationalism because she believed it destroyed international workers' solidarity, Luxemburg was appalled when her fellow socialists supported the war in 1914. She and **Karl Liebknecht (1871-1919)** formed a pacifist faction of the SPD, the **Spartacists**, and were imprisoned for demonstrating against the war. When she was released in November 1918, she helped transform the Spartacists into the **German Communist party**.

In her 1917 book *The Russian Revolution*, Luxemburg denounced the excessively centralized structure of **Vladimir Lenin's (1870-1924) Bolshevik party** and the terror that followed the **Russian Revolution**. Instead, she advocated the use of spontaneous, mass political strikes as the main instrument of revolution. In contrast to Lenin, she believed that "the dictatorship of the proletariat consists in the application of democracy not in its abolition."

Arrested in January 1919 for taking part in an unsuccessful Spartacist uprising, she and Liebknecht were then seized by anti-Communist German soldiers, who first interrogated and then executed them. Luxemburg's body was thrown into the **Landwehr Canal**. Her murderers were later acquitted.

Maria Montessori.

Born in Chiaravalle, Italy, **Maria Montessori** enrolled in engineering at the University of Rome, but graduated with an M.D. in 1894, becoming Italy's first woman doctor. While at the university's psychiatric unit, she developed a unique educational program that prepared mentally handicapped children to pass the state exam in reading and writing for eight-year-olds. In 1901, she held the hygiene chair at the **Scuola di Magistero Femminile,** and from 1904 to 1908 she was a professor of anthropology at Rome University and worked as a government school inspector.

Before beginning her work with normal children, Montessori examined educational systems in Europe and found that children were "reduced to immobility" in classrooms, placed in rows like "butterflies transfixed with pins." Such children, she declared, were not "disciplined but annihilated." As she saw it, the task of the educator was in "seeing that the child does not confound good with immobility and evil with activity." In 1907, she applied her methods to normal children aged three to six at a **Casa dei Bambini (Children's House)**—a set of rooms set aside for children in the courtyard of tenement buildings—in Rome's San Lorenzo slum district. The children, whose parents were illiterate, learned to read, write and do simple addition. In 1912, Montessori's book *The Montessori Method* described these techniques. Her 1917 book, *Advanced Montessori Method*, detailed her work with children aged six to 10. In contrast to traditional methods, which use a formal process of rewards and punishments, Montessori's method uses a spontaneous learning process and stresses the development of individual initiative and self-reliance by allowing children to move freely and pursue what interests them within a clearly defined framework of acceptable behavior.

Montessori teachers act as guides and supervisors rather than as directors of a set curriculum. They give a child individual instruction and introduce new material as required. When movements are involved, the teacher models them first so a child can learn good habits. The Montessori system also stresses sensory perception and developing motor coordination through the use of activities, games and simple yet stimulating objects that capture children's interest and make them want to explore further.

Montessori spent her later years lecturing and supervising training programs and published *Education for a New World* in 1946. She died at Noordwijk in the Netherlands at the age of 82.

Julia Morgan, whose trailblazing career helped open the field of architecture for American women, was raised in Oakland, California. In 1890, she became the first woman student at the University of California at Berkeley, College of Engineering. After graduating in 1894, she performed drafting work with **Bernard Maybeck** before becoming the first woman admitted to the Architectural Section of the Ecole des Beaux-Arts in Paris. In 1898, she was its first woman graduate.

After Morgan became the first woman to receive a state architect's license, **Phoebe Hearst** hired her to remodel her residence in Pleasanton, California, and to collaborate with Maybeck on a family retreat. In the aftermath of the **1906 San Francisco earthquake** and fire, Morgan firmly established her reputation by rebuilding the once-elegant **Fairmont Hotel**. She also designed **St. John's Presbyterian Church**, which became an architectural landmark in Berkeley, and several buildings for **Mills College**, a women's institution located in Oakland.

Although Morgan worked in a variety of styles, her favorite was **Spanish Revival**. Many of her commissions came from women and women's institutions, such as the **Young Women's Christian Association (YWCA)**, for whom she designed buildings in Salt Lake City, Honolulu and throughout California and their **Asilomar Conference Center** near Monterey. Although Morgan was not a politically active feminist, she did hire numerous women architects and draftspeople and anonymously provided financial aid to women students.

In 1919, newspaper publisher **William Randolph Hearst (1863-1951)** commissioned Morgan to design a castle retreat on the family ranch at **San Simeon** midway between San Francisco and Los Angeles, instructing her to incorporate sections of European castles that he had already purchased. She also designed facilities for his offices in San Francisco and Los Angeles and private residences in California and Mexico. These commissions constituted one-third of Morgan's workload for the next 20 years.

Morgan's career reached its height in the late 1920s when she built the **Berkeley City Club** and with Maybeck laid out the entire campus of **Principia College** in Elsah, Illinois. In her lifetime, she designed 800 structures.

Acknowledging that she was a decade ahead of most contemporaries in the use of structure as a means of expression, architectural scholars recognize Morgan as one of the prime style innovators of the western United States during the first half of the twentieth century. She died of a stroke in San Francisco at the age of 75.

Julia Morgan.

The first freeborn member of a slave family of 17 children from Mayesville, South Carolina, **Mary McLeod Bethune** went on to become one of the most influential African-American women of the twentieth century. During the post-Reconstruction era, few blacks had access to education, but Bethune was able to attend mission schools and become a teacher. Believing that education was the primary route to black advancement, in 1904 she founded the **Daytona Educational and Industrial Institute** in Daytona Beach, Florida, with "five little girls, a dollar and a half and faith in God." She conducted the institute in a "head-heart-hand" tradition, offering academic and religious training while having her students work an adjacent farm to provide the school's food.

From the start, the charismatic Bethune forged a bond with both black and white community leaders and received their financial support. In 1923, she merged her school with the coeducational Cookman Institute to form **Cookman-Bethune College**. In 1943, the college awarded its first degrees in elementary education. This accomplishment made her the first woman of her generation to found an institution for disadvantaged youth that became a four-year college.

This success was the springboard for Bethune's leadership in the black women's club movement. Through the **National Association of Colored Women (NACW)**, she strove to give black women an effective voice in public affairs and she made NACW a vital force in the essentially white **International Council of Women**. In 1935, she founded the **National Council of Negro Women (NCNW)**, a lobbying vehicle for social concerns. In 1941, she made NCNW part of the **Women's Interest Section (WIS)** of the War Department, one of the few federally sponsored settings for female leadership. As an assistant to the Secretary of War, Bethune insured that the **Women's Army Auxiliary Corps (WAAC)** allotted 10 percent of its officer candidate spaces to blacks.

From 1936 to 1944, Bethune was director of Negro Affairs in the **National Youth Administration (NYA)**, a government slot higher than that held by any other black woman in the history of the country up to that time. Enjoying unrestricted access to the White House and close personal relationships with both **Franklin Roosevelt (1882-1945)** his wife **Eleanor Roosevelt** (see page 81), she was able to secure federal funding for vocational training and jobs for black youth, which helped pave the way for black pilots in the military. Bethune also served as a consultant on interracial affairs at the charter conference of the **United Nations**. She died of a heart attack at the age of 80.

Mary McLeod Bethune.

A pioneering advocate for the rights of the handicapped, **Helen Keller** was born in Tuscumbia, Alabama. Trapped in a silent, dark world after an illness left her deaf, dumb and blind at the age of 19 months, she became a willful, destructive child. When she was seven, her family hired **Anne Sullivan (1866-1936)**, a recent graduate of the Perkins Institute for the Deaf, as a teacher and governess. After only two weeks a breakthrough occurred when Helen understood the word "water" Anne signed into her hand, and a lifelong bond was forged between her and "Teacher."

In 1900, Keller entered Radcliffe College. Sullivan accompanied her to all of her classes and signed the lectures into her hand. When the *Ladies Home Journal* asked Helen to write her autobiography, Sullivan hired Harvard professor John Macy to assist them. *The Story of My Life* appeared in 1902. In 1904, Helen graduated *cum laude*. Sullivan and Macy were married the following year, remaining together until 1913.

Helen Keller.

In 1906, when New York established its first **State Commission for the Blind**, the governor appointed Keller to it, and she and Macy crisscrossed the country to raise funds. Keller also launched a campaign against *ophthalmia Neonatorum*—blindness in infants—becoming the first person to speak out about how venereal disease, which was preventable, caused this and other devastating illnesses. Later that year, **Mary Agnes Thomson (1885-1960)** joined their household as a live-in housekeeper.

In 1924, the **American Foundation for the Blind (AFB)** made Keller its spokesperson. She also continued to be active in the many social reform movements, including the abolition of child labor and capital punishment. After Macy died in 1936, Thomson became Keller's compan-

ion. In the 1930s, Keller effectively lobbied in Washington on behalf of AFB, helping to obtain federally funded reading services and talking books for the blind, and she was instrumental in having the blind included as as grant category under Title X of the **Social Security Act**.

During **World War II**, Keller made morale-building tours of military hospitals, and in the 1950s she undertook lecture tours in South Africa, the Middle East and Latin America on behalf of the visually handicapped. After Thomson's death in 1960, Keller retired from public life. In 1964, she was awarded the **Presidential Medal of Freedom** by **President Lyndon Johnson (1908-1972)**.

Keller's books include *The World I Live In* (1908), *Out of the Dark* (1913), *Midstream—My Later Life* (1930), *Let Us Have Faith* (1940), *Teacher: Anne Sullivan Macy* (1955) and *The Open Door* (1957). She also made two documentary films about her life, *Deliverance* (1918) and *Helen Keller in Her Story* (1954).

America's first female cabinet member, **Frances Perkins** is remembered as a champion of the nation's working class. Born in Boston, Massachusetts, she attended Mount Holyoke College then taught for several years before receiving her M.A. in economics at Columbia University in 1910. While living in Chicago, she worked at **Hull-House** settlement house, where she had her first experience with labor unions when she helped workers collect back wages.

As secretary of the **New York Consumers' League** (1910-1912), Perkins drew attention to sweatshop conditions. After witnessing the 1911 **Triangle Shirtwaist Company** fire that killed 146 workers, she became committed to lobbying for protective labor laws. In 1912, she went to work for the New York State Committee on Safety, exposing unsafe conditions and proposing corrective legislation, such as limiting the work week to 54 hours.

In 1913 Perkins married economist **Paul Wilson** but retained her maiden name. In 1918, governor **Alfred E. Smith (1873-1944)** appointed her to an $8000-a-year job on the New York State Industrial Commission, making her the highest-paid state employee in the nation. In 1926, Smith made her industrial commissioner for the state, a position she continued to hold between 1929-1932 under Smith's successor, **Franklin D. Roosevelt (1882-1945)**.

When Roosevelt was elected president in 1932, he chose Perkins as his **Secretary of Labor**, calling her "his most loyal friend," and she was to be one of only two original cabinet appointees to serve from 1933 until his death in 1945. As his **New Deal** policies took shape, Perkins helped draft legislation that was to impact American domestic policy for the next 50 years, including the **Federal Emergency Relief Act**, the public works section (Title II) of the **National Industrial Recovery Act**, the **Civilian Conservation Corps Act**, the **National Labor Relations Act** and the **Social Security Act**.

Not only did Perkins help construct New Deal policies, but she tirelessly and skillfully helped to implement them across the country. She also restructured the Department of Labor, ridding the **Immigration and Naturalization Service** of racketeers and establishing the **Division of Labor Standards**. In all instances, her pro-labor stance was evident as she sought to promote the welfare of wage earners.

After Roosevelt's death, Perkins served on the **Civil Service Commission** under President **Harry S. Truman (1884-1972)** from 1945 until 1953, and at age 77 she became a professor at Cornell University's School of Industrial Relations, where she taught until she died of a stroke in New York City.

Frances Perkins.

Like **Hypatia** (see page 17), mathematician **Amalie Emmy Noether** was the daughter of a mathematician and university professor. Most well known for her work in **abstract algebra**, she grew up in the university town of Erlangen, Germany, where her father often gathered Emmy and her three younger brothers around him to explain mathematics problems. When the University of Erlangen opened its doors to women, she became one of only two females among 1000 students, graduating with high honors in 1907 with a Ph.D.

Although German universities admitted women as students, they still did not allow them to become professors. For the next eight years, Noether lived at home, and as her father became increasingly ill, she often taught his classes—without pay—as a substitute teacher. In 1916, **David Hilbert** and **Felix Klein**, who were working on Einstein's **Theory of Relativity** at the University of Gottingen, invited her to join their research group. When the university refused to hire a woman, Hilbert made it possible for her to lecture—again, without pay—by announcing her lectures under his own name. Noether, who had a unique ability to work with abstract concepts and visualize complex connections, gained the respect of both the students and faculty. In 1920, she presented a paper on the building up, on an axiomatic basis, of a completely general theory of ideals, a work that was to mark her unique contribution to abstract algebra.

After Adolf Hitler came to power in Germany in 1933, Noether emigrated to the United States and accepted a professorship at Bryn Mawr College near Philadelphia. She also worked at the Institute for Advanced Studies at Princeton University. When she died unexpectedly of complications following routine surgery at the age of 53, **Albert Einstein (1879-1955)**, who had used her work on the **Theory of Invariants** in formulating some of his relativity work, eulogized her by calling her "the most significant creative mathematical genius thus far produced since the higher education of women began."

Emmy Noether.

73. MARGARET HIGGINS SANGER
1883-1966

Margaret Higgins Sanger.

Birth control pioneer **Margaret Higgins Sanger** was born in Corning, New York, the sixth of 11 children. Watching her mother's endless struggle to raise a large family on a small income and her early death at age 49 fueled Sanger's commitment to securing access to reproductive choice for all women. She attended nursing school at White Plains Hospital, and in 1902 she married **William Sanger**, an architect, with whom she had three children in their eight years of marriage.

While working as a midwife and visiting nurse in New York, Sanger became active in the **International Workers of the World's (IWW)** effort to organize textile workers. Following the death of a young client from a self-induced abortion, Sanger focused her efforts on the issue of reproductive autonomy and vowed to establish a nationwide system of advice centers where women could obtain reliable birth control information.

Her militant journal, *Woman Rebel,* launched in 1914, led to an indictment for violating the postal code. She also distributed a pamphlet, *Family Limitation,* which contained detailed information on birth control techniques. In October 1916, Sanger and her sister **Ethel Bryne** opened a clinic in the Brownsville section of Brooklyn, providing 488 women with contraceptive advice over 10 days before the clinic was closed by police. The ensuing trial of the "birth control sisters," which charged Sanger with "maintaining a public nuisance," made her a national figure. She was convicted but won an appeal, opening the way for physicians to give birth control advice in the city of New York.

In 1921, Sanger founded the **American Birth Control League**, a national lobbying organization, and served as its president until 1928. In 1941, the League became the **Planned Parenthood Federation of America.** In 1927, she organized the first **World Population Conference.** Her **Birth Control Clinical Research Bureau**—the first doctor-staffed clinic in the United States—opened in New York in 1923. The Bureau also served as a teaching facility for doctors. In 1936, Sanger realized one of her life's goals when a federal judge's ruling in the case *United States v. One Package* overturned the notorious **1876 Comstock Act**'s classification of birth control as "obscenity," making it possible for doctors to teach contraception in medical schools. She chronicled her life story in her 1938 book *An Autobiography.*

After **World War II**, Sanger founded the **International Planned Parenthood Federation** and served as its first president. Her efforts also led to the introduction of the first birth control pill in 1960. She died of heart failure in Tucson, Arizona.

74. ELEANOR ROOSEVELT
1884-1962

Probably the most influential and effective woman in twentieth century American politics, First Lady and social activist **Eleanor Roosevelt**, more than any woman of her generation, exemplified the personal and political autonomy that were the goals of the women's rights movement. Born in New York City, a niece to President **Theodore Roosevelt (1858-1919)**, she attended Allenwood, an exclusive boarding school near London. In 1901, after making her society debut, she joined the **National Consumer's League**, evaluating safety conditions in sweatshops, an experience through which she developed a lifelong commitment to political activism.

In 1905, she married her distant cousin, **Franklin Delano Roosevelt (1882-1945)** and they had five children. Beginning in 1910, when he was elected to the New York Assembly, Eleanor was active in politics. She coordinated the legislative program for the state **League of Women Voters** and worked with the **Women's Trade Union League (WTUL)** to pass minimum wage laws. When Franklin was paralyzed by polio in 1921, she saved his political career by organizing newly franchised women voters in the state Democratic party to help elect him governor. By 1928, when she led the national women's campaign for the Democratic party, she had become a respected political leader in her own right.

During Franklin's first of four successful presidential campaigns in 1932, Eleanor coordinated the women's division of the **Democratic National Committee**. A tireless advocate for the rights of women, minorities and the disadvantaged, in her first year as First Lady she traveled over 50,000 miles. She strongly supported the women's division of the **Civil Works Administration**, which provided 100,000 women with jobs, as well as the **National Youth Ad-**

Eleanor Roosevelt.

ministration, the **Social Security Act** and measures to end racial discrimination in the armed forces. In January 1936 she began a syndicated newspaper column, **My Day**, to share her views. She also prompted her husband to hire qualified women for his administration, such as **Frances Perkins** (see page 78), leading one newspaper columnist to call Eleanor a "Cabinet Minister without portfolio—the most influential woman of her time."

After her husband's death, President **Harry S. Truman (1884-1972)** appointed Eleanor as a delegate to the **United Nations (UN)**. In 1948, the UN passed the Universal Declaration of Human Rights, a document largely shaped by her, and the entire delegation gave her a standing ovation. Her last official position was to chair the **Commission on the Status of Women** for President **John Kennedy (1917-1963)** in 1961. She is the author of *It's Up to Women* (1933) and *This, I Remember* (1949). She died in New York City at the age of 78.

Born in Hamburg, Germany and educated at the University of Berlin and the University of Freiburg, child psychoanalyst **Karen Horney** was an instructor at the Berlin Institute for Psychoanalysis for two years before emigrating to the United States in 1932. After serving as an associate director of the Chicago Institute for Psychoanalysis from 1934 to 1941, she taught at the New York Psychoanalytic Institute. In 1941 she co-founded the **American Institute for Psychoanalysis** and served as its dean. The next year she joined the staff of the New York Medical College.

Horney founded a **Neo-Freudian school of psychoanalysis** which stressed that early childhood conflicts and deprivation can lead to neuroses in adulthood. In contrast to Sigmund Freud who stressed the biological basis of neuroses, Horney, a **learning theorist**, believed that the environmental and social aspects of a child's experience played the key roles in personality development.

In her books, *The Neurotic Personality of Our Time* (1937) and *New Ways in Psychoanalysis* (1939), Horney made **basic anxiety** her primary concept. She believed that basic anxiety occurs if a child is treated with coldness and extreme inconsistency by those who raise him. As a result, a child may attempt to cope with these feelings in inappropriate or maladjusted ways. If his anxieties are intense and prolonged, a child's maladaptive methods can become fixed in the form of **neurotic needs**, which Horney defined as being "excessive, insatiable and unrealistic demands for affection, approval, someone to depend on, power or personal achievement."

Horney also challenged popular notions about the nature of **masochism** which claimed that the reason many women were abused by their mates was because they somehow preferred such treatment. She was the first of her profession to state that so-called "natural" feminine masochism was more likely to be the result of a sexist societal system of rewards and punishments that encouraged women to act in extremely passive or overly submissive ways.

Her Freudian male colleagues did not appreciate her views and forced her out of the **New York Psychoanalytic Society**. Yet by the 1970s, most mental health professionals came to agree with Horney's viewpoint. She died of abdominal cancer at the age of 67.

Karen Horney.

76. SISTER ELIZABETH KENNY
1886-1952

A pioneer in the use of **physiotherapy** who revolutionized medical treatment for polio victims, **Sister Elizabeth Kenny** was born at Kelly's Gully near Warialda in New South Wales, Australia. She first became interested in nursing at the age of 14 when her frail younger brother sent away for "The Great Sandow's Muscle Course" and she helped drill him in the body-building exercises.

Kenny received only limited formal education as a child, but in her late twenties she decided to study nursing, though she was never certified. When she first began working with patients paralyzed by polio in the Australian bush country in 1911, she was not familiar with the orthodox treatment for the disease, which consisted of immobilizing limbs with casts and splints. Instead, Kenny obtained good results by applying hot blankets and moving, massaging, manipulating and "re-educating" the muscles of the polio victims. Her methods served to lessen deformity and taught patients how to best use the muscles left intact.

During World War I, she worked as an army transport nurse, tending to wounded soldiers on ocean voyages home, and earned the title of "Sister"—as nurses in British Empire countries were called. After the war, she developed a canopied stretcher on wheels to shuttle the sick across the rugged Australian outback.

In 1933, during one of the frequent polio epidemics, people asked for her help and Kenny set up a table under an awning in Townsville. News of her success spread quickly. Although conservative doctors criticized her lack of formal education and dismissed her techniques, the governments of New South Wales and Queensland set up a series of "Kenny clinics." In 1940, she traveled to the United States, where she was given an opportunity by the **National**

Sister Elizabeth Kenny.

Foundation for Infantile Paralysis (NFIP) (later the **March of Dimes Foundation**) and the University of Minnesota to lecture and demonstrate her methods at Minneapolis General Hospital. Many doctors, who had become dissatisfied with the results they obtained using traditional methods of immobilizing children in casts and frames, became convinced that Kenny's method did indeed offer a better treatment, particularly in the early stages of the disease.

In 1941, the NFIP's medical advisory committee officially endorsed Kenny's treatment. In 1942, after the **American Medical Association** approved, the **Elizabeth Kenny Institute** was founded in Minneapolis to train nurses and **physiotherapists** in her techniques. She died in Toowoomba, Queensland, Australia, at the age of 66.

11. LOUISE BOYD
1887-1972

Explorer **Louise Boyd** was born in 1887, one of three children of San Francisco mining magnate **John Franklin Boyd**. Left a wealthy heiress at age 30 with no close relatives, she decided to travel. In 1924, she chose a most extraordinary destination: **Spitsbergen**, a small archipelago in the Arctic Sea between Norway and East Greenland, stating she had always been "fond of geography from earliest childhood" with a special interest in "northern latitudes."

On her 1924 trip, the first of seven expeditions Boyd led to the Arctic, she became the first woman to set foot on **Franz Josef Land**, where she made a photographic documentation of every aspect of the landscape. The focus of her 1928 trip became a 10,000-mile, three month search for explorer **Roald Amundsen (1872-1928)**. Although her search proved fruitless, she was decorated by the king of Norway with the **Order of St. Olaf**, becoming the first non-Norwegian woman to receive this honor. In 1930, she embarked on a two-month trip to the extreme northern regions of Scandinavia to collect botanical specimens and photograph the native people of the area, the **Lapps**.

In 1931, Boyd undertook a scientific exploration of the fjords of **East Greenland**, making detailed surveys of typical small areas. Her close study of every fjord and sound in the Franz Josef-King Oscar fjord area revealed errors in previous mappings. Inner reaches of the Ice Fjord that she charted were named **Miss Boyd Land**. The results of her 1933 expedition were published as *The Fjord Region of East Greenland*. On her 1937 outing, Boyd mapped another new region, which was named **Louise Boyd Bank**. Her greatest triumph came during her 1938 expedition when she landed her steamship *Veslekari* farther up the East Greenland shore than any other

Louise Boyd.

American ever had. Calling her "the only woman to achieve an outstanding position in Arctic exploration," the **American Geographical Society** awarded her the **Cullum Medal** in 1938 and elected her to the **Council of Fellows**, the first woman in its 108-year history to be so honored. Details of her explorations can be found in E.F. Olds' book *Women of the Four Winds* (1985).

During **World War II**, the US government considered Boyd's data to be of such strategic military importance that she had to postpone publication of her book, *The Coast of Northeast Greenland*, until 1948. She also served as a consultant to military intelligence in Washington in 1942. When she died at the age of 84, at her request, her ashes were scattered over the Arctic.

Poet and diplomat **Lucila Godey Alcaya** (pen name: **Gabriela Mistral**) was born in the Elqui Valley village of Vicuna in northern Chile and brought up by her mother, a schoolteacher. From this humble beginning, she became one of the most celebrated and influential South American writers of the twentieth century and a symbol of the nationalist aspirations of her country.

After studying education, child welfare and labor issues, Mistral taught in rural secondary schools and in 1912 she became the director of the Liceo de Los Andes in Punta Arenas in southern Chile. Upon publication of her first book, *Sonetos de la Muerte* in 1914, she became known for her poetry, which critics said displayed a "visionary, prophetic sense of the destiny of Latin America." In 1922, her collection *Desolacion* appeared, and she was also

Lucila Godey Alcaya.

sent by the government to study educational and library systems in Mexico for two years, where she collaborated on a national educational reform program. Upon her return home, she was honored for her work. Later that year, *Ternura* was published.

In 1925, Mistral began a second career as a diplomat when she was named as the Chilean delegate to the **United Nations**, where she became head of the **Cultural Committee** and the **Committee of the Institute of International Intellectual Cooperation** in Paris between 1926 and 1939. After serving as the **Chilean Consul** in Madrid in 1934, she was made a "life consul" and later worked in posts in Lisbon, Nice, Rio de Janeiro and Los Angeles. In 1944, she was diagnosed as being diabetic and moved to the United States for her health, where she served as a cultural attache. Following a 13-year hiatus in her writing, Mistral published two books of poems *Tala* (1938) and *Lagar* (1954). She also wrote several novels about Chilean life. In her many books, theses and poems, Mistral seemed devoted to an intellectual and spiritual quest. As M.A. de Vasques relates in the book *Gabriela Mistral: The Poet and Her Work* (1964), Mistral was haunted by grief from the suicide of her first love in 1909 and that of her nephew, whom she had adopted, and thus her work, "while reflecting deeply private feelings, seemed to speak with a voice that all humanity could understand." Although she closely identified with her country, once stating, "I am and will remain, a daughter of my land," she nonetheless acknowledged the influences from diverse sources, including Spanish, Russian and Indian writers, and Christian and Buddhist philosophers.

In 1945, Gabriela Mistral became the first South American writer to receive the **Nobel Prize for literature**.

AGATHA CHRISTIE
1891-1976

Born in Torquay, England, celebrated mystery author and playwright **Agatha Christie** was a prolific writer who, over a span of more than 50 years, penned 68 novels, 17 plays and more than 100 short stories that have been published in 103 languages throughout the world. She first became interested in mystery stories as a young girl when her sister Madge introduced her to the adventures of **Sir Arthur Conan Doyle's (1859-1930)** cerebral sleuth Sherlock Holmes and then dared her to write a baffling mystery of her own. The result was *The Mysterious Affair at Styles*, which appeared in 1920 when Christie was 29. Christie's stories are well-known for their lively cast of colorful characters and intricate plots twists. She also invented two very memorable detectives. **Hercule Poirot** (pwä′rō), an eccentric Belgian detective who solves puzzles presented to him by using his "little gray cells" to make deductions, first appeared in *The Mysterious Affair at Styles*. When Christie killed off Poirot in *Curtain* (1975), his death made the front page of the *New York Times*. **Miss Jane Marple**, Christie's other well-known sleuth, was an elderly spinster who ferreted out murderers in her small village of St. Mary's Mead. She made her debut in 1930 in *Murder at the Vicarage* and continued her pursuit of elusive murderers until her final appearance in *Sleeping Murder* (1976), which was published after Christie's death.

On a trip to the Middle East in 1930, Christie met her second husband, archaeologist **Sir Max Mallowan (1904-1978)**. She subsequently accompanied him on his yearly digs in Iraq and Syria. From these travels sprang her novels *Murder in Mesopotamia* (1930), *Death on the Nile* (1937) and *Appointment with Death* (1938). *Agatha Christie: An Autobiography*, appeared in 1977.

Christie's play, *The Mousetrap*, which opened at the Ambassador Theater in London in 1952, has been continuously performed ever since, making it the world's longest-running theatrical production. Her play, *Witness for the Prosecution* (1953), received the **New York Drama Critics' Circle Award** in 1954. In 1971, **Queen Elizabeth II (b. 1926)** appointed her a Dame of the British Empire.

Agatha Christie.

80. MARTHA GRAHAM
1894-1991

Martha Graham.

The most influential and innovative figure in modern dance for over 50 years, **Martha Graham** was born in Pittsburgh, Pennsylvania, but grew up in California. At age 20, she studied ethnic and primitive dance at the Denishawn School in Hollywood, where director **Ted Shawn**, recognizing her remarkable talent, created the ballet *Xochitl* on an Astec theme for her. From 1923 to 1925, she danced in the *Greenwich Village Follies*, and in 1926 she taught at the Eastman School of Music, where she began to explore how dance could "give substance to the things she felt."

Graham launched her career as an independent dancer and choreographer in a solo debut at the **48th Street Theatre** in New York that shocked and amazed the audience. Unlike traditional ballet, Graham's movements were angular, taut and low to the ground, and consisted of intense thrusts of movement outward from the center of her body to express emotions. She founded the **Dance Repertory Theater** and quickly established a reputation for providing the most strenuous training in the field. Her unique teaching method emphasized contracting and releasing different parts of the body and using breathing in relationship to movement.

Graham's works centered on the universal experiences of humankind and on the themes of love, death and the cyclical nature of life. From 1928 to 1938—which she called "the period of long woolens"—she choreographed works on protest themes such as *Revolt, Immigrant, Lamentation* and *Primitive Mysteries*. In 1932, she became the first dancer to receive a Guggenheim fellowship. She created a number of dances based on famous women such as Joan of Arc and Mary, Queen of Scots and explored in depth the psyches of Emily Dickenson (*Letter to the World*,

1940) and the Brontë sisters (*Deaths and Entrances*, 1943). Greek drama and myth inspired *Cave of the Heart* (1946) about Medea; *Night Journey* about Oedipus' mother, Jocasta; and the first full-length modern dance work ever written, *Clytemnestra* (klĭ'təm-nes'trə) (1958). After 1938, she used music only expressly composed for her dances by such famous composers as **Aaron Copland (b. 1900)** (*Appalachian Spring*, 1944) and **Gian-Carlo Menotti (b. 1911)** and **Samuel Barber (1910-1981)**.

Graham, who choreographed 180 works and enjoyed the longest active career of any modern dancer, retired from the stage in 1969 to become a full-time teacher, lecturer and director of the **Martha Graham Center for Contemporary Dance** in New York. She received numerous honors, including the **Presidential Medal of Freedom** in 1976. She died in New York City at the age of 97.

81. ANNA FREUD
1895-1982

Born in Vienna, Austria, the daughter of the founder of psychoanalysis, **Sigmund Freud** (froid) **(1856-1939)**, **Anna Freud** is most well-known for her pioneering work in the field of child psychoanalysis. After working as a children's teacher, she collaborated with her father on the development of **Psychoanalytic Theory**. In her method, which came to be known as the **Vienna School**, the therapist interprets the meaning of the child's play to the child and greater emphasis is placed on the therapist's educational role with the family.

In 1938, Anna and her father fled to England to avoid Nazi persecution, where after Sigmund's death Anna continued to utilize and expand upon his theories. In 1945, she helped to launch the annual periodical *Psychoanalytic Study of the Child*, and in 1947 she opened the **Hampstead Child Therapy Course and Clinic** in London, later serving as its director in 1952. The term "defense" was first used by Sigmund Freud in 1894 to describe the ego's struggle with pain. But it was only with Anna Freud's *The Ego and Mechanisms of Defense* (1946) that **defense mechanisms** achieved the importance they deserved in both theory and therapy. This ground-breaking book marks the beginning of **Ego Psychology**. Psychoanalysts turned from concentrating solely on interpreting the unconscious to the patient to placing an equal emphasis upon discovering and interpreting the various defense mechanisms which a patient uses to avoid feeling pain or anxiety. According to Freud, defense mechanisms include: denial, repression, introjection, projection, displacement, reaction formation, isolation, undoing, regression, fixation and intellectualization.

Freud stressed that all defense mechanisms also had a positive side and are a necessary part of everyone's personality development. She believed they became

Anna Freud.

harmful to a person's psychological well-being only when overused, at which point they can distort a person's view of reality and impede further healthy psychological growth.

Freud also studied the nature of **separation anxiety** in infants (*Infants Without Families*, 1944) and feeding disorders (1946), the latter of which she classified into "organic," "nonorganic disturbances of the instinctive process itself" and "neurotic feeding disturbances." Many aspects of her work also extended to family law, where she emphasized the importance of the psychological bond between a parent and child.

Upon her first return to Vienna in 1971, she was given a standing ovation at the 27th International Psychoanalytical Congress. The following year, Vienna University became one of many institutions to award her an honorary doctorate.

Daring American aviatrix **Amelia Earhart** (âr′härt) became a national heroine in 1928 when she became the first woman to cross the Atlantic Ocean by air. She later chronicled her experience in *20 Hours, 40 Minutes* (1928). She dropped out of Columbia University to earn money for flying lessons and worked as the aviation editor at *Cosmopolitan* magazine. She founded the **Ninety-Nines**, an international organization of women pilots. Though her flying career was brief, her numerous accomplishments—including being the first woman to receive the **Distinguished Flying Cross**—still stand as an inspiration.

Earhart was only a passenger on that first historic flight, having accepted an invitation from pilots **Wilmar Stutz** and **Louis Gordon** to accompany them on their transatlantic journey, but in 1932 she became the first woman to fly solo over the Atlantic. Her time of 13 hours, 30 minutes set a record, for which she was awarded honors by both the American and French governments. In 1935, she became the first woman to fly over the Pacific Ocean when she crossed from Hawaii to California. Later that year, she set a speed record flying nonstop from Mexico City to New York City in 14 hours, 19 minutes.

On May 21, 1937, accompanied by navigator **Fred Noonan**, her husband **George Putnam (1887-1950)** and mechanic **Bo McNeeley**, Earhart took off from Oakland, California, in a **Lockheed Electra Model 10E**. Her intention was to become the first woman to circumnavigate the globe by circling the equator. When the plane refueled in Miami, Putnam and McNeeley left the flight, and Earhart and Noonan continued on, flying east.

In 1987, **Carol Osborne**, with Earhart's sister **Muriel Earhart Morrissey** wrote *Amelia, My Courageous Sister*. According to Osborne's research, which included numerous personal interviews, Earhart took off from Lae, New Guinea, on July 1, 1937 heading toward Howland Island. Radio experts aboard the *Itasca*, a US Coast Guard ship awaiting her arrival, picked up this transmission: "We are circling but cannot hear you." Due to the strength of the signal, *Itasca* personnel believed she was close to Howland. An hour later at 8:46 a.m. Howland time, after Earhart had been in the air 20 hours, 16 minutes, she sent her last transmission: "We are on the line position 157-337…are running north and south."

When Earhart's plane disappeared, the Navy conducted an exhaustive search of the area until July 18, but to this day, no wreckage has ever been found. What happened? Many theories have been advanced over the years, but Earhart family members and Osborne maintain that Amelia's plane ran out of fuel and she and Noonan died at sea. However, despite Osborne's well-researched book, Earhart's disappearance remains one of the most intriguing mysteries of the twentieth century.

Amelia Earhart.

83. GOLDA MEIR
1898-1978

An stateswoman of incomparable stature and the first woman prime minister of Israel, **Golda Mabovitch** was born in Kiev in the Ukraine, then emigrated to Milwaukee, Wisconsin, in 1905. She attended the Teachers Training College in 1917 and in the same year married **Morris Myerson** (later modifying this name to the Hebrew, **Meir**). Active in the **Labor Zionist party**, she and her husband emigrated to Palestine (later Israel) in 1921, where they joined the **Kibbutz Merchavia**. In 1923, they settled in Tel Aviv and she worked as a treasurer in the Office of Public Works of the **Histradruth**, the labor federation.

In 1928, Meir became secretary of the **Women's Labor Council** in Palestine and was elected as a delegate to congresses of the **World Zionist Organization**. After serving on the **Jewish National Council**

Golda Meir.

and on the board of directors of several Histradruth aid programs, in 1940 she was appointed head of the Histradruth's political department. She continued in this role until Israel's independence was declared on May 14, 1948, when, as a member of the **Provisional Council of State**, she became one of the signers of Israel's **Declaration of Independence**. She then served as the first Israeli minister to the USSR for six months.

In January 1949, Meir was elected to the first Israeli *Knesset* (Parliament) as a *Mapai* (Labor) representative, and Prime Minister **Ben Gurion** appointed her **Minister of Labor and Social Insurance**, making her the only woman in his administration. While in this office, she successfully resolved the sensitive issues of housing and employment for the mass of immigrants pouring into the newly formed Jewish state. In 1956, she became **Minister of Foreign Affairs**, a position she held for 10 years. Meir also chaired the Israeli delegation to the **United Nations** from 1953 to 1966. For the next two years, she served as the secretary-general of the Labor Party, and during this time she was able to reunite the three main Labor party elements: *Mapai, Achdut Ha'Avodah* and *Rafi*. Eight months after the merger, she retired from political office.

Upon the death of prime minister **Levi Eshkol** in March 1969, Meir was asked to act as an interim prime minister and went on to be elected to the office in October of that year. During the next six years, she built a solid international reputation as a tough-minded but empathetic leader. She resigned in 1974 after controversy arose over Israel's lack of preparedness for the Yom Kippur War of October 1973. Her autobiography, *My Life*, was published in 1975. She died in Jerusalem at the age of 80.

Anthropologist **Margaret Mead**'s (mēd) father was a professor of economics at the University of Pennsylvania and her mother was a sociologist who had studied Italian immigrants. At Barnard College, she was influenced by anthropologists who believed that patterns of behavior were culturally transmitted (**"nurture"**) rather than genetically inherited (**"nature"**).

In the summer of 1925, Mead went to **Ta'u Island** in **American Samoa** to conduct a field study. For nine months she interviewed natives about their family life and sexual behavior. Her book, *Coming of Age in Samoa* (1928), strongly supported "nurture" as being the major determinant of human behavior. Until Mead's study, the role of women in society, child-rearing practices and questions about how values and traditions were handed down from one generation to the next had been largely ignored by anthropologists. Her book not only secured her reputation as a nationally prominent intellectual, but its frank advocacy of sexual freedom, though written in a scientific context, made it a bestseller.

Mead conducted several other field studies, including one of the **Manus** people of the **Admiralty Islands** near **New Guinea** (*Growing Up in New Guinea*, 1930), where, to measure the mental functioning of children, she pioneered the use of psychological tests such as drawings. She is considered the founder of the **Nature and Personality School of Anthropology**, which focuses on the ways cultures shape personality, and she advanced the documentary use of photography and later video.

In 1926, Mead became the assistant curator of ethnology at the **American Museum of Natural History** in New York, holding various posts there until becoming a Curator Emeritus in 1970. From 1948 to 1950, she was director of research in con-

Margaret Mead.

temporary cultures at Columbia University and an adjunct professor after 1954. In 1969, she became a full professor and head of the social science department at Fordham University. In the 1960s and 1970s, she was a frequent interview guest on radio and television and gave numerous lectures.

Using a jargon-free, novelistic style of writing, Mead produced over two dozen works, including *Sex and Temperament in Three Primitive Societies* (1935), *Male and Female* (1949), *Culture and Commitment: A Study of the Generation Gap* (1970) and her autobiography *Blackberry Winter* (1972).

On November 15, 1978, the day the *World Almanac* named her one of the world's 25 most influential women, Margaret Mead died of pancreatic cancer in New York City at the age of 77.

85. MARIAN ANDERSON
1902-1993

Born in Philadelphia, Pennsylvania, the daughter of a coal and ice merchant, contralto **Marian Anderson** was destined to become a legend not only for her magnificent, three-octave voice, but also as the first African-American opera singer to break the barrier of racial prejudice.

Anderson began singing in her church choir at age six, and at age 22 she entered a vocal contest, which she won over 300 other singers, giving her the opportunity to perform with the **New York Philharmonic Orchestra**. She embarked on a European concert tour culminating at the 1935 Salzburg Festival in Austria, where conductor **Arturo Toscanini (1867-1957)** welcomed her by exclaiming that her voice was "such as one hears once in a hundred years."

Marian Anderson.

Although she returned to America as an internationally renowned celebrity, Anderson was still relegated to performing in segregated halls. In 1939, the **Daughters of the American Revolution (DAR)** would not allow her to present a recital in Philadelphia's Constitution Hall, claiming that the date she requested had already been taken. When First Lady **Eleanor Roosevelt** (see page 81) learned of this, she resigned from the organization and arranged for Anderson to give an open-air concert at the **Lincoln Memorial** in Washington, DC, on Easter Sunday. Her performance, which included spirituals, Schubert's *Ave Maria* and the national anthem, drew more than 75,000 people, the largest public tribute since **Charles Lindbergh (1902-1974)** returned home a decade earlier.

Although she felt ill-at-ease prior to singing that day, as she wrote in her 1956 autobiography *My Lord, What a Morning*, "I could see that my significance as an individual was small in this affair. I had become, whether I liked it or not, a symbol, representing my people. I had to appear."

President **Franklin Roosevelt (1882-1945)** later invited Anderson to sing for King George VI at the White House, making her the first black artist to sing there. In January 1955, she made her debut with New York's **Metropolitan Opera**, opening the way for an entire generation of black artists, including **Leontyne Price, Jessye Norman** and **Kathleen Battle**.

In 1958, President **Dwight Eisenhower (1890-1969)** appointed her to the Human Rights Committee of the United Nations, and in 1961 she sang at **John F. Kennedy's (1917-1963)** inauguration. In 1963, she received the **Presidential Medal of Freedom**. In April 1993, one month after suffering a stroke, she died at her home in Danbury, Connecticut, at the age of 91.

86. MARGARET BOURKE-WHITE
1904-1971

Considered the leading American woman photojournalist of the twentieth century, **Margaret Bourke-White** (bûrk' hwīt') was born in New York City, the second child of an engineer-designer. She entered Rutgers University at 17 to study engineering and biology and graduated from Cornell University in 1927, where she supported herself by selling idyllic pictures of campus life.

Like many photographers of the 1920s and 1930s, Bourke-White's work celebrated machines and the technological age. In 1927, she moved to Cleveland, where she specialized in architectural and industrial subjects, which she described as "sincere and unadorned in their beauty." In 1929, she joined the staff of the new magazine *Fortune*, beginning a lifelong association with the publications of **Henry R. Luce (1898-1967)**, which included *Time* and *Life* magazines. The direction of her career changed dramatically after she produced a social documentary piece for *Fortune* on the Midwest's drought-stricken **Dust Bowl** (*The Drought*, October 1934). Moved by what she saw, she began to photograph the human experience.

In 1935, Bourke-White joined the staff of Luce's new showcase for photojournalism, *Life* magazine. Sent to cover a Montana dam project, on her own initiative she produced a human interest piece on nearby frontier towns. Luce subsequently used this material for the cover picture and lead article in the first issue of the magazine on November 23, 1936.

That same year Bourke-White collaborated with writer **Erskine Caldwell (b. 1903)** on a haunting portrait of Southern sharecroppers. Considered a landmark documentary, *You Have Seen Their Faces* (1937) is her most historically significant work. During their brief marriage between 1939 and 1942, they also produced *North*

Margaret Bourke-White.

of the Danube (1939) on Czechoslovakia before the war and *Say, Is This the U.S.A.* (1941).

During **World War II**, Bourke-White became a war correspondent with the US Army Air Force. Often present on the front line of battles, she accompanied General **George Patton (1885-1945)** and the Third Army to record the last days of the **Third Reich**. Entering the death camps, she produced *The Living Dead of Buchenwald*, a classic in the history of photography. Bourke-White's postwar assignments included India and the Korean War, where she focused on the human interest aspects rather than guerrilla fighting. By the mid-1950s, she had reached the peak of her profession. After she contracted Parkinson's Disease, she documented her rehabilitation as an encouragement to others. She died in Stamford, Connecticut. Her autobiography, *Portrait of Myself*, was published in 1963.

87. RACHEL CARSON
1907-1964

When she was a young girl growing up in Springdale, Pennsylvania, **Rachel Carson** was greatly influenced by her mother, **Maria Carson**, a schoolteacher who shared her deep love of nature with her. Later, as a marine biologist committed to preserving the beauty of the earth, she wrote *Silent Spring* (1962), a landmark book which focused the attention of the world on environmental dangers and helped launch the environmental protection movement.

After graduating *magna cum laude* from Pennsylvania College for Women, Carson received an M.A. from Johns Hopkins University in 1932. She worked summers at the **Marine Biological Laboratory** in Massachusetts and in 1935 became one of the first two women staff biologists at the **US Bureau of Fisheries**. Her 1937 article for *The Atlantic Monthly*, entitled *Undersea*, later became her first book, *Under the Sea-Wind* (1941).

During **World War II**, Carson worked for the **US Fish and Wildlife Service**, and by 1949 she was chief editor of their publishing program. Her second book, *The Sea Around Us* (1951), first serialized in *The New Yorker* magazine, became an immediate bestseller, won the **National Book Award** and was eventually translated into 32 languages.

After years of struggling to financially support her mother and two orphaned nieces, Carson received a Guggenheim Foundation fellowship in 1951, which allowed her to take a year's leave of absence from her job. Her next book, *The Edge of the Sea* (1955), solidified her reputation as an articulate interpreter of natural science. In 1957, after her niece died, Carson adopted her five-year-old son, **Roger Christie**, who served as an inspiration for a 1956 magazine article, *Help Your Child to Wonder*. The article was published after

Rachel Carson.

her death as an illustrated children's book, *The Sense of Wonder*.

The precipitating event to Carson's most famous work, *Silent Spring*, was a request for help from a friend who had witnessed the wholesale destruction of wildlife in her bird sanctuary after it had been sprayed with pesticides. Using data gathered from scientists throughout America and Europe, Carson wrote a searing indictment of the indiscriminate use of toxic chemicals and the irresponsibility of industrialized societies toward the earth and its resources. As a direct result of her exposé, President **John Kennedy (1917-1963)** formed a special panel to study the effects of pesticides on the environment.

Rachel Carson died of bone cancer in 1964 in Silver Spring, Maryland. By 1972, the United States government had banned all domestic use of DDT.

Agnes Gonxha Bejaxhia was born to Albanian parents in the town of Skopje, Macedonia. At the age of 18, she entered the Roman Catholic Order of the **Sisters of Our Lady of Loretta** in Ireland. After she received training in Dublin and Darjeeling, India, she took her vows.

In 1929, as **Sister Teresa**, she became part of a group of Loretta nuns in Calcutta and taught high school there for nearly 20 years. While working as a teacher, she was deeply moved by the incredible suffering of the sick and dying she encountered daily on the crowded city streets. On September 10, 1946, while riding a train in Darjeeling, she received what she believed to be a clear call from God to leave the Sisters of Loretta and to devote her life to working for the impoverished of the city while living among them.

Granted permission by the Pope to leave her post at the convent, in 1948 Mother Teresa began her lifelong ministry among the poor. Two years later, she and her workers were approved by the archdiocese of Calcutta as the new order of the **Missionaries of Charity**. The order was later recognized as a Pontifical congregation under the direct jurisdiction of Rome. Women joining this religious community took four vows upon acceptance. In addition to the traditional clerical vows of poverty, chastity and obedience, Missionaries of Charity took a fourth vow pledging service to the poor.

The basic belief underlying Mother Teresa's work was that the poor symbolized Christ and that by serving them, she and her sisters were serving Christ. The sisters saw their primary mission as a religious one, although they carried out their work in various ways as nurses and social workers.

In 1952, Mother Teresa opened the **Nirmal Hriday (Pure Heart) Home for Dying Destitutes** in Calcutta. Since that time, she has extended her work to five continents. Her book about her life, *Gift from God*, was published in 1975. In recognition of her achievements, she was awarded the **1975 Nobel Prize for Peace**, and in 1985 she received the **Presidential Medal of Freedom** from the United States.

Mother Teresa.

89. ROSA PARKS
b. 1913

Rosa Parks.

Known as the first lady of civil rights, **Rosa Parks'** refusal to give up her bus seat to a white man sparked the **Montgomery bus boycott** in 1955, which was the catalyst for the **American civil rights movement** of the 1960s.

Born in Tuskegee, Alabama, she married barber **Raymond Parks** in 1932. In 1943, she was one of the first women to join the Montgomery chapter of the **National Association for the Advancement of Colored People (NAACP)**, where she served as a youth advisor and secretary from 1943 to 1956, as well as office manager for State President **Edgar Nixon**.

In 1955, Montgomery public buses were segregated by law. On Thursday, December 1, 1955, Parks, who was on her way home from her tailoring job, was sitting in the first row of the designated black section. When a white man boarded, the bus driver asked four blacks to move. Three did; Rosa Parks refused. The driver called the police, who arrested and jailed her.

Because 75 percent of the bus ridership was black, African-American community leaders decided that a boycott would make a powerful economic impact and Parks agreed to allow her December 5 trial to become the focus of the fight against segregation. On December 2, 52,000 fliers were distributed calling for a one-day bus boycott on the day of her trial. The boycott was so successful, it was continued indefinitely. After Parks was found guilty and fined $10, she refused to pay and appealed her conviction.

Parks and her husband soon lost their jobs, and she then helped organize carpools to maintain the boycott. Though blacks were harassed and threatened, the boycott continued. In 1956, after the **Montgomery Improvement Association** filed suit, the United States District Court declared that segregated seating on public buses was un-constitutional, a decision upheld by the United States Supreme Court. After 381 days, the bus boycott had ended in success.

In 1957, Parks moved to Detroit, Michigan, where she continued her civil rights work with the **Southern Christian Leadership Conference (SCLC)**, which since 1963 has annually sponsored the **Rosa Parks Freedom Award**. Between 1965 and 1988, she worked as a staff assistant to US Representative **John Conyers**. The recipient of many honorary degrees and awards, Parks was the first woman to receive the **Martin Luther King Nonviolent Peace Prize** (1980), and the city of Detroit named a boulevard and arts center in her honor. In 1987, she established the **Rosa and Raymond Parks Institute for Self-Development** to work with teens. In 1990, 3000 government and community leaders gathered at the Kennedy Center in Washington, DC, to celebrate her 75th birthday.

Named the "greatest woman athlete of the first half of the twentieth century" in a 1950 Associated Press poll, women's sports pioneer **Mildred Ella Didrikson** (dĭd′rĭk-sən) was born in Port Arthur, Texas, the fourth of seven children of Norwegian immigrants. Her father was a carpenter and her mother was a practical nurse and amateur athlete.

Didrikson's performance on the Beaumont High School basketball team caught the attention of **Melvin McCoombs**, who recruited her for his company-sponsored AAU team. After the team won the national championship, Didrikson took up track. She competed in eight events in the 1932 **National AAU Track & Field Championships**, winning five, tying one and accumulating enough points to win the team championship by herself. At the **1932 Olympics** in Los Angeles, limited to three events, she became an **Olympic gold medalist** and set records in the javelin (143 feet, 4 inches) and the 80 meter hurdles (11.7 seconds), and won a silver medal for high jump.

Didrikson next took up golf and won the **Texas Women's Championship** in 1934. Less than a month later, she was ruled ineligible for amateur competition because she had accepted money in other sports. In 1938, Didrikson married wrestler **George Zaharias** and regained her amateur status. She then won an unprecedented 17 consecutive golf tournaments, including the **US Amateur Championship, World Championship** and the **US Women's Open**. In 1947, she became the first American to win the **Women's British Open**.

Following this success, Didrikson turned professional. With her husband's advice and financial support, she began to lay the groundwork for professional women's competition in golf. In 1948, she and five other women golfers created the **Ladies Professional Golf Association,** recruiting a sporting goods company as a sponsor for the initial set of tournaments. Didrikson's tenacity of spirit showed itself when she was stricken with cancer. In 1955, just 15 months after major surgery, she won her third Women's Open title.

A gifted athlete, Didrikson's talent and widespread popularity helped to dispel existing myths about the competitive ability of women athletes, thus opening the door for more women to compete in a wider variety of professional sports. Didrikson's autobiography, *This Life I've Led*, was published in 1955. The following year her cancer recurred and she died at the age of 42.

Mildred "Babe" Didrikson Zaharias.

91. INDIRA GANDHI
1917-1984

One of the most tenacious and influential political leaders of her time, India's first woman prime minister **Indira Priyadarshini Nehru** was born in Allahabad, the only child of **Jawalharlal Nehru (1889-1964)**, India's first prime minister. After attending school in Switzerland and England, she married childhood friend and journalist **Feroze Gandhi (d. 1960)**. Upon returning to India in 1942, they were imprisoned for 13 months for their support of the nationalist movement. They had two sons, Rajiv and Sanjay.

Growing up, Gandhi had known most of the leaders of the nationalist struggle for freedom, including **Mohandas "Mahatma" Gandhi (1869-1948)** (no relation). After Britain granted independence to India in 1947, she served as her father's hostess and confidant for 18 years until his death in 1964. Throughout this time she was active in numerous social and political organizations, serving as chairperson of the **Central Social Welfare Board** (1953-1957) and president of the **All India Youth Congress** (1956-1960) and was a member of the **Congress Working Committee** and the **Central Election Committee**. When her father died, she was elected to his seat in Parliament. In 1964, Prime Minister **Lal Shastri** appointed her **Minister of Information and Broadcasting**. When he died two years later, she was elected leader of the Congress Party and became India's third prime minister. After party members opposed to her policies split the party, Gandhi called a general election in 1971, tirelessly touring the country to gain public support, and was elected by a large margin.

At the peak of her power, Gandhi experienced a series of setbacks. Growing economic difficulties sparked demonstrations in 1974 and she declared Emergency Rule, imprisoning political adversaries and severely censoring the press, measures seen by some as violating the Constitution. In the March 1977 elections, she was turned out of office. In October 1977, she was jailed briefly on charges of official corruption, and 14 months later she was expelled from Parliament. Following this, she reorganized her party and was re-elected prime minister in a landslide victory in the election of January 1980.

On the world front, Gandhi became a forceful spokesperson for Third World and developing nations, but she continued to face sectarian opposition at home. In 1983 and 1984, she sent government troops to quell disturbances in the Punjab, and they sacked the **Sikh** (sēk) temple. In retaliation, Gandhi was assassinated by two of her Sikh bodyguards at her residence in New Delhi in June 1984. Her son Rajiv was immediately sworn in as prime minister.

Indira Gandhi.

Known to many as the mother of the modern women's movement, **Betty Goldstein** was born in Peoria, Illinois. Her mother was a journalist who abandoned her career when she married—a fact that played a key role in the development of Friedan's feminist beliefs. She studied at Smith College and the University of California at Berkeley. In 1947, she married **Carl Friedan** (frĭ-dăn′), a theatrical producer, and became a full-time homemaker for their three children. Feeling unfulfilled while living the supposedly ideal life of a suburban New York housewife, Friedan wrote her now classic 1963 book, *The Feminine Mystique*, which debunked the 1950s myth of the "happy homemaker." It sold 65,000 hardback and 700,000 paperback copies in the first year. When *Mystique* appeared, the average age for women to marry in the United States was 19.8 years and 93 percent had been married by age 30. Friedan identified "the problem that has no name" as resulting from the "feminine mystique"—the stereotype perpetuated by society, and reinforced in the press, that the only rewarding role for a woman was to sacrifice her individual self identity and submerge herself in the role of a wife and mother. The result, Friedan asserted, was that in middle age many women felt empty. She recommended that women seek professional careers where they could use their intellect and talents.

Friedan was one of many twentieth century women to articulate the issue of women's constricted role in society. In 1941, **Pearl Buck** (1892-1973)—winner of the Nobel Prize for *The Good Earth* (1938)—wrote *Of Men and Women*. Although this book went largely unnoticed because it appeared in November 1941, it exposed the myth that women had freedom and opportunity and called for equal access in education and work. Another book

Betty Friedan.

which traced the nature of women's oppression through the ages was the massive two-volume study *The Second Sex* (1949) by French philosopher and author **Simone de Beauvoir (1908-1986)**, which appeared at a time when most women were content with postwar affluence. Friedan's book became a catalyst for the women's liberation movement because it appeared in the 1960s, a decade of massive social change when women were ready to take action. In 1966, Friedan founded the **National Organization for Women (NOW)** to ensure the adoption and enforcement of women's rights legislation, serving as president until 1970. She also helped organize the **National Women's Political Caucus** in 1971, led the 1970 **National Women's Strike for Equality**, convened the **International Feminist Congress** in 1973 and helped found New York's **First Women's Bank** the same year. Her other works include *The Second Stage* (1981) and *Fountain of Age* (1993).

Shirley St. Hill Chisholm, an outspoken and independent legislator, in 1968 became the first African-American woman to be elected to the **United States Congress**. Four years later, she became the first black person of either gender to seek a major party nomination for president.

Born in the Bedford-Stuyvesant section of Brooklyn, New York, Chisholm and her sisters went to live with their maternal grandmother in Barbados for seven years while her impoverished parents saved money for their children's futures, as they strongly believed in the importance of education. Chisholm studied to be a teacher at Brooklyn College, graduating *cum laude*, and received an M.A. in early childhood

Shirley Chisholm.

education at Columbia University, where she met and then married **Conrad Chisholm**.

In 1953, having worked as a teacher in a child care center and as director of a nursery school, Chisholm joined the **New York City Bureau of Child Welfare**. She also became active with the **Seventeenth Assembly District Democratic Club**, where she helped form the **Unity Democratic Club** to work for reforms in the district's political machine. In 1964, she ran for the New York State Assembly and won by a comfortable margin of 18,151 to 1893 and 913 votes in a three-way contest.

After Congressional district lines were redrawn in 1968, Chisholm ran for the seat from the new, primarily black, twelfth district. She won by 1000 votes and went on to be re-elected six more times before she retired in 1982. While in the **House of Representatives**, she earned a reputation as a maverick, often crossing party lines when voting. At the 1972 Democratic Convention, she received 151 delegate votes in her bid against George McGovern for the party nomination.

In 1982, Chisholm became a professor at Mount Holyoke College, and in 1985 she was a visiting scholar at Spelman College. In 1984, she founded the **National Political Congress of Black Women (NPCBW)**, and in 1988 the group sent a delegation of 100 women to the Democratic Convention to present demands for promoting civil rights and social programs. Instead of for her "firsts," Chisholm would rather be remembered "as a catalyst for change, a woman who had the determination...and perseverance to fight on behalf of the female population and the black population, because I'm a product of both..." In 1993, President **Bill Clinton (b. 1946)** appointed her United States ambassador to Jamaica.

Britain's first woman prime minister, **Margaret Roberts Thatcher**, was born in Grantham, Lincolnshire, England, the daughter of a prominent grocer and Methodist lay preacher who twice served as town mayor. In 1947, she graduated from Somerville College at the University of Oxford with a degree in chemistry, and for the next four years she worked as a research chemist for a Colchester plastics firm and for J. Lyons & Company.

When she was 22, she pursued her first public office as a candidate in Dartford. In 1951, she married **Denis Thatcher**, who managed his family's paint business, and left her job to pursue a degree in law, taking her bar finals in 1953 after an unusually short time. That same year she gave birth to twins, a son and a daughter. Afterward, she worked as a tax lawyer until she won a seat in Parliament for Finchley, London in 1959.

From 1961 to 1964, she served as **Joint Parliamentary Secretary** for the **Ministry of Pensions and National Insurance**, and became **Secretary of State for Education and Science** when her party won the election. In 1974, she was elected leader of the **Conservative party**, and in 1979 she led her party to victory, becoming the first woman prime minister in Britain's history. Thatcher once expressed her philosophy of leadership thusly: "There can be no liberty unless there is economic liberty... Extinguish free enterprise and you extinguish liberty." Her fiscal policies included attacking inflation by reducing the money supply, reducing public spending and raising interest rates. In 1982, her hard line stance at home, as well as abroad—as evidenced by her outspoken stand against the USSR's invasion of Afghanistan— earned her the nickname of **The Iron Lady**. The quick military intervention that she ordered following Argentina's invasion

Margaret Thatcher.

of the **Falkland Islands** in 1982 also won her high praise.

Thatcher's second term of office in 1983 was marked by confrontations with major unions. Her policies led to a reduction in the inflation rate from 24 percent in 1979 to 3.5 percent and her encouragement of privatization programs led to the creation of several major public companies, such as British Gas and British Airways.

In 1987, Thatcher became the first British prime minister in the twentieth century to win three consecutive terms, and she came to be regarded as an elder stateswoman, having built close ties with other major world leaders. In 1990, after losing support within her own party, she resigned as prime minister, although she continued to serve in Parliament until 1992. Her autobiography, *The Downing Street Years*, was published in 1993.

Before the full force of Nazi persecution befell them, **Anne Frank** and her family moved from their home in Frankfurt, Germany, to Amsterdam in the Netherlands, where her father, **Otto Frank**, established a food products business. After 16-year-old **Margot Frank** was summoned for deportation in July 1942, the Franks went into hiding in a **"secret annex"** on the second floor of an Amsterdam commercial building. They were joined by Frank's business associate, **Mr. Van Daan**, his wife and their 15-year-old son **Peter**, and **Albert Dussel**, an elderly dentist. Sustained by Dutch friends who supplied food and other essentials, the group succeeded in eluding detection for 25 months by remaining still during the day and moving about only at night after workers downstairs had gone home. It was in this claustrophobic environment that Anne Frank's extraordinary chronicle of adolescence took shape.

Shortly before their ordeal began, Anne had received a diary for her thirteenth birthday on June 12, 1942. Addressing her diary as **"Dear Kitty,"** she recorded, with great wit and perception, the daily routine in the annex and her dreams for the future. The hopes of the group were greatly bolstered when they heard that the Allies had invaded France. Surely the war would soon be over!

The last entry in Anne's diary was August 1, 1944. Betrayed by a worker in the office below for the usual reward of five gulden ($1.40) per person, the eight Jews were arrested three days later. On the day that the Allies liberated Brussels, Belgium, they were among the last shipment of a thousand people to leave Holland. At **Auschwitz** in Poland, the men and women were separated. It was the last time Otto Frank—the only one of the annex group to survive—ever saw his family.

After the war ended in 1945, Frank re-

Anne Frank.

turned to Amsterdam, where his Dutch protectors gave him Anne's diary, which they had found in the annex. In 1947, it was published as *Het Achterhuis* (The Secret Annex), and in 1952 it appeared in English as *Anne Frank: Diary of a Young Girl*. The play, which opened in New York in 1955, won a **Pulitzer Prize** for its authors.

Through interviews with 42 people who had known Anne, **Ernest Schnabel**, author of *Anne Frank, A Portrait in Courage* (1958), learned that she had died of typhoid in the **Belsen** concentration camp shortly before it was liberated. "Her voice was preserved," Schnabel wrote, "out of the millions that were silenced, this voice no louder than a child's whisper... It has outlasted the shouts of the murderers and has soared above the voices of time."

96. TONI MORRISON
b. 1931

Toni Morrison, whose visionary work about African-Americans and the sufferings of the human condition makes her one of the most significant writers of the twentieth century, received the **1993 Nobel Prize in literature** for her book *Jazz*. Morrison was the first black, and only the eighth woman, to win the prize since it was first awarded in 1901. Born in Lorraine, Ohio, as **Chloe Anthony Wofford**, her most vivid memories of her childhood include learning about black folklore, music and myths, and storytelling, which was a major source of family entertainment. She graduated from Howard University in 1953 with a degree in English and changed her name to **Toni**. In 1955, she earned a masters degree from Cornell and then taught at Texas Southern University. Two years later she returned to Howard and married architect **Harold Morrison**.

In 1956, Morrison became a textbook editor for Random House Publishing in Syracuse, New York, and in 1959 she moved to New York City as a senior editor in its trade department. While there, she continued her teaching career at State University of New York at Purchase (1969-1970), Yale University (1975-1977) and Bard College (1979-1980). Her first novel, *The Bluest Eye*, about a young girl's yearning for unattainable physical beauty, appeared in 1970. By the end of the decade she had written *Sula* (1974), about the 20-year friendship of two girls in the 1920s, and *Song of Solomon* (1977), for which she received the **National Book Critics Circle Award** and an appointment to the American Academy and Institute of Arts and Letters. The following year, President **Jimmy Carter (b. 1924)** appointed her to the **National Council of the Arts**. In 1984, she left publishing to become the humanities chair at the State University of New York at Albany, where she remained until ac-

Toni Morrison.

cepting the Robert Goheen Professorship on the Council of the Humanities at Princeton, becoming the first black woman writer to hold a named chair at an Ivy League university.

Morrison has received more than 15 honorary degrees and numerous honors and awards, and her biography was featured in the PBS series *Writers in America*. Her other works include *Tar Baby* (1981), which made her the first black American woman to appear on the cover of *Newsweek* magazine; *Beloved* (1987), a moving account about the harsh legacy of slavery, for which she received the **Pulitzer Prize**; the play *Dreaming Emmet*; and a book of essays, *Playing in the Dark* (1992). Morrison said she was inspired by "things that had never been articulated, printed or imagined...about black girls, black women. I don't want to redress wrongs. I want to alter the language and rid it of...its racism and fill the void with the voice of black women. It is a risky business."

The first woman president of the Republic of the Philippines, **Corazon Cojuangco Aquino** served a six-year term between 1986 and 1992. Assuming leadership of a country whose economic wealth had been depleted during the corrupt 20-year dictatorship of **Ferdinand Marcos (1917-1989)**, she succeeded in establishing, preserving and ultimately handing over to a hand-picked successor a working democracy.

The daughter of a congressman and grand-daughter of a senator, Aquino was born on her family's sugar plantation in Tarlac province. Educated at private Catholic schools and in Philadelphia and New York, she set aside her law studies in 1956 when she married **Benigno Aquino (d. 1983)**, who later became leader of the opposition to the Marcos regime. In 1972, when Marcos declared martial law and arrested his adversaries, Benigno was imprisoned, and for the next seven years Corazon acted as a liaison to his followers. In 1980, Benigno was released for heart surgery in the United States, after which the Aquinos and their five children lived near Boston for three years.

In August 1983, Benigno returned to Manila, where he was gunned down by government loyalists as he left his airplane. After 26 defendants were acquitted of his murder, Corazon became active with the opposition, traveling the country to rally people and to demand Marcos' resignation. Urged repeatedly to run for president, she agreed to do so in her husband's place when it became clear that she alone was popular enough to win. Using intimidation and sabotage, the 1986 election was rigged by Marcos supporters. However, a bloodless "people's revolution," led by Lieutenant General **Fidel Ramos (b. 1928)**, deputy chief of the armed forces, declared Corazon to be president, and Marcos fled the country.

Sworn in as the seventh president of the Philippines on February 25, 1986, she immediately abolished the National Assembly and organized a commission to draft a new constitution modeled after that of the United States. She governed by decree and through local and national appointees until a new congress was elected in 1987. Although she had been faced with vast debts, entrenched political corruption, an ongoing guerrilla war between the army and Communist insurgents, attacks from Marcos backers and seven attempted coups by the military—the last of which in 1989 provided the final setback to the economic revival of the previous three years—Corazon's anointed successor, Fidel Ramos, became president after peaceful national elections in May 1992. Aquino had accomplished what she had set out to do.

Corazon Aquino.

Cosmonaut **Valentina Tereshkova** (tə-rĕsh-kō′və) was born on a farm near the village of Maslennikovo, Russia. Her father, a tractor driver, was killed in **World War II**. After working in a tire factory, she joined her mother and sister to work in a cotton mill. She was an active member of the **Young Communist League**, and in 1959 she took up parachute jumping as a sport, quickly becoming proficient. By the time she entered the space program, she had completed 126 jumps.

In 1961, inspired by the pioneering space flight of **Yuri Gagarin** (gə-gär′ĭn) Tereshkova wrote the government to volunteer for the space program. After completing the rigorous physical and technical cosmonaut training on June 16, 1963, she became the first woman to be launched into space. Once aloft, she sent this transmission back to earth: "This is Seagull. I see the horizon. A light blue, a blue band. This is the earth. How beautiful it is. Everything goes fine."

In her craft, the *Vostok VI*, she completed 48 orbits over a period of three days, traveling a total of 1,225,000 miles. Soviet President **Nikita Krushchev** (kr o͞o sh′ch ə v) **(1894-1971)** named her a **Hero of the Soviet Union** and awarded her the **Order of Lenin** and the **Gold Star Medal**. Taking the

opportunity to chastise the West for their "bourgeois" attitude that women were the "weaker sex," Krushchev pointed out that on her historic flight, Tereshkova had remained in space longer than all four male American astronauts combined.

In 1963, Tereshkova married fellow cosmonaut **Andrian Nikolayev** and they had a daughter, **Yelena**, in 1964. Her birth aroused great interest because she was the first child born to parents who had both been in a space environment. Tereshkova continued her career as an aerospace engineer, traveling abroad to lecture about her experiences in space. In 1977, she became chairperson of the **Soviet Women's Committee**, and in 1987 she became head of the **Union of Soviet Societies for Friendship with Foreign Countries**.

Valentina Tereshkova.

The founder of the **Children's Defense Fund (CDF), Marian Wright Edelman** is esteemed as the leading voice for children's rights in America. Born in Bennettsville, South Carolina, she was the daughter of a Baptist minister who expected his children to get an education and then use it to serve their community. At Spelman College, she received stipends to study at the Sorbonne in Paris, the University of Geneva, Switzerland and the Soviet Union. In 1960, she became active in the civil rights movement, participating in a mass sit-in at the Atlanta City Hall, where she and 13 other students were arrested. This experience proved to be a turning point for Edelman, who abandoned a career in international relations to become a civil rights lawyer.

After graduating as valedictorian in 1960, Edelman entered Yale University Law School. In 1963, she worked on a voter registration drive in Mississippi, and after graduation she became one of the first two National Association for the Advancement of Colored People (NAACP) interns in Jackson, Mississippi. Between 1964 and 1968, while continuing her civil rights works in private practice, she headed the NAACP Legal Defense and Educational Fund. In 1968 she married **Peter Edelman**, a Harvard Law School graduate, and they had two sons. Edelman realized that in order to effect systemic changes, she had to impact federal policy. Using a grant to study how to make laws work for the poor, she started the **Washington Research Project**. In 1971, she became director of the Harvard University Center for Law. In 1973, she founded the CDF with the goal of securing long-term, fundamental services for children and making children's needs an urgent national priority. Edelman viewed CDF's mission as educating Americans about how to take preventative action in the areas of health, education, child care, youth employment, child welfare and family support services. In 1987, CDF was responsible for introducing the Act for Better Child Care. Its 1993 lobbying efforts centered on child care and early childhood education.

Edelman has served on numerous boards, including that of Spelman College, and commissions, such as the National Commission on the International Year of the Child (1977). She has received over 35 awards from organizations—ranging from the National Women's Political Caucus, to Big Sisters and the Albert Schweitzer Humanitarian Prize (Johns Hopkins, 1988)— and over 40 honorary degrees. She is the author of many articles, including *In Defense of Children's Rights* (1978), as well as several books, such as *Children Out of School in America* (1974) and *Families in Peril: An Agenda for Social Change* (1988).

Marian Wright Edelman.

100. RIGOBERTA MENCHU
b. 1959

A Quiche Mayan Indian born in the remote northern highlands of Chimal, Guatemala, **Rigoberta Menchu** (mĕn' shōō), winner of the **1992 Nobel Peace Prize**, became one of the most powerful voices for the rights of indigenous peoples in the Americas. Growing up, she witnessed the brutality perpetrated by government forces on her people—which make up 60 percent of the country's population of 9.2 million. During Guatemala's civil war, the longest-running leftist rebellion in the history of the Americas, more than 100,000 people died in mass killings in the 1980s.

As a child, Menchu traveled with her father, activist **Vincente Menchu**, a founding member of the **Committee of Peasant Unity (CUC)**. In her 1984 autobiography, *I Rigoberta Menchu: An Indian Woman in Guatemala*, she described how her father was burned to death with other protesters when government security forces stormed the Spanish Embassy in Guatemala City, and how she and her mother watched in silence—so as not to be killed themselves—as soldiers tortured and immolated her 16-year-old brother and other "subversives." After her mother was murdered and her two sisters joined the guerrillas, Menchu went into exile in Mexico in 1981.

In exile, Menchu continued to forcefully condemn the intolerable human rights conditions in her country, working with the CUC to focus world attention on the plight of indigenous peoples in Guatemala and other countries in the Americas, including the United States. She also was a vocal critic of American support of Guatemala's military regime, which in the early 1990s still averaged two "extrajudicial executions" or forced disappearances every day.

With the $1.2 million Nobel Prize money, Menchu founded the **Vincente Menchu Foundation** to help Indian street

Rigoberta Menchu.

children and the widows of murdered political prisoners and to promote projects that preserve Mayan culture. While applauding the efforts of the **United Nations** to resettle refugees and help mediate Guatemala's civil war, she cautioned that because the conflict in Guatemala was of long standing and deeply rooted in the extreme polarization of rich and poor, it would take a long time to resolve

For Menchu, the key issues in ending her country's strife were eliminating the oppression of Indians by Ladinos (persons of mixed blood), allowing Indians to maintain their own culture and creating a society based on mutual respect and equal participation. "I have the Nobel Peace Prize in exile with me in Mexico," she said in 1993. "It will stay there as part of a vigil for Guatemala...until we can make a pilgrimage [home] with it one day."

TRIVIA QUIZ & GAMES

Test your knowledge and challenge your friends with the following questions. The answers are on the pages listed.

1. At the first American women's rights convention in Seneca Falls, New York in 1848, a document was introduced which made the first public demand for voting rights for women. Which two women organized the convention? What was the name of the document? Who wrote it? (See page 46)

2. What is "physiotheraphy?" Who pioneered its use to treat polio victims? (See page 83)

3. At dawn on the morning of August 24, 1572, the worst slaughter in the history of France began. It later came to be known as the St. Bartholomew's Day Massacre and eventually claimed 50,000 lives. Name the queen responsible and her reason for such a drastic measure. (See page 25)

4. Who were the "Spartacists" and what did they oppose? (See page 73)

5. Two popular English queens lent their names to historical eras. Who were they? (See pages 26 and 51)

6. There are many women who are known by the "firsts" they achieved. Name the following trailblazers: a) the "first modern feminist" b) the "first woman mathematician" c) the "first woman doctor in Scotland" (See pages 35, 17 and 61)

7. Who is considered to be the pioneer of smallpox inoculation in Europe? (See page 29)

8. In the 1980s, the US Department of Defense named its new systems implementation programming language after this early computer programming pioneer. What was the name of the program? For whom was it named? (See page 45)

9. Twenty-nine of the women discussed in this book spent all, or part, of their careers in the teaching profession. Name at least 10. (See pages 10, 11, 17, 30, 42, 43, 44, 47, 52, 55, 56, 57, 60, 61, 69, 73, 74, 76, 78, 79, 82, 85, 87, 88, 89, 91, 100 and 103)

10. In conjunction with her husband, which woman scientist's work on the characteristics of heat and fire helped lay the foundation for modern chemistry? (See page 34)

11. How much did Lewis and Clark pay the young Shosone Indian Sacajawea for her services as a guide and interpreter on their 1804 expedition up the Missouri River? (See page 39)

12. In the context of the American women's rights movement of the nineteenth century, what was a "Stoner?" (See page 49)

13. Because of their courageous acts and exceptional bravery, these seven women came to be considered national heroines in their countries. Who were they? (See pages 9, 16, 22, 40, 53, 58 and 89)

14. Who was the first woman African-American self-made millionaire and what products did she market? (See page 70)

15. Five women in this book had statues dedicated in their honor—one by an ardent admirer and four by the governments of their countries. Name the women and who was responsible for erecting their memorials. (See pages 12, 14, 53, 58 and 64)

16. What was the "Underground Railroad?" Who founded it? (See page 54)

17. What causes the condition known as "phossy jaw?" What did this and other intolerable industrial working conditions lead to? (See page 62)

18. What is the name of the oldest existing piece of Jewish literature? Who is said to be its author? (See page 9)

19. Nobel Prizes have been awarded yearly since 1901 for merit in physics, chemistry, medicine and physiology, literature and world peace. (Economics was added in 1969.) Name the women and years of the following awards: physics (1) (See page 69), chemistry (2) (See page 69), literature (3) (See pages 85, 99 and 103) and peace (4) (See pages 55, 67, 95 and 107). Which woman was the first to receive a Nobel Prize and the only one to receive two? (See page 69)

20. What incident proved to be the catalyst for the American civil rights movement of the 1960s? (See page 96)

21. Upon her death in 1872, what writer of scientific texts was acclaimed by the London Post as "The Queen of Nineteenth Century Science?" (See page 38)

SUGGESTED PROJECTS

1. In 1923, three years after the Nineteenth Amendment granted American women the vote, Carrie Chapman Catt wrote: "It is doubtful if any man...ever realized what the suffrage struggle came to mean to women... How much time and patience, work, energy, aspiration, faith, hope and despair went into it. It leaves its mark on one, such a struggle." What was the first country to grant women the vote? What was the most recent? Are there still places in the world today where women either have a limited access, or no access at all, to the right to vote?

2. Both Maria Montessori and Catherine Beecher were pioneers in the field of education. How do Montessori's learning methods differ from those used in traditional preschools or elementary schools? How many of Beecher's innovative ideas are actually in use today in modern classrooms?

INDEX